JOE FISON

A man afire with God

AFIRE FOR GOD

The Life of Joe Fison

by

F. W. Dillistone

with a Foreword by
Lord Coggan

Oxford
The Amate Press
1983

Contents

Foreword

There are two reasons why I feel privileged to write a *Foreword* to this book. The first is that I knew Joe Fison from the early thirties to the time of his death and, though our paths crossed only rarely, I had a deep respect and affection for him. Though he has been dead some eleven years, many who knew him will want to read his *Life,* and many who did not know him will be inspired by his story.

My second reason is that the writing of this *Foreword* gives me the opportunity of paying my tribute to the author of the book. Dr. Dillistone has put great numbers of people in his debt by giving them the substantial biographies of Charles Raven, C. H. Dodd and Max Warren. This is a slighter book, but is to be welcomed none the less eagerly for that.

As with his other biographies, Dr. Dillistone has approached his subject with great sensitivity. It is not easy to trace the growth of a soul, particularly of one so rare as that of Joe Fison. I believe Dr. Dillistone has succeeded in doing just that. To read of that growth has been me a moving experience, and I believe others, particularly those who find that that growth has involved them in pain, will be similarly moved and helped.

"The goodly fellowship of the prophets praise thee". Joe Fison belonged to that fellowhsip. We who read this biography join in their praise to God.

Donald Coggan

Preface

I shall never forget the first time I set eyes on Joe Fison. It was in October 1925. He was standing in the middle of New Inn Hall Street in Oxford, lifting up his voice, while a little group of undergraduates around him were sharing in the merriment. That was the beginning of a friendship which lasted until his death in 1972. Over considerable periods we saw nothing of one another but from the time he became Bishop of Salisbury in 1963 we were often able to meet.

I have written this memoir out of affection but also with a growing feeling of admiration. His ability to win his way into people's hearts was phenomenal. His capacity to apply familiar texts, especially those of the Bible, to contemporary life in fresh and arresting ways was remarkable. His unswerving ambition to be identified with Christ in word and deed was truly apostolic.

I know of only one other Bishop this century who could be compared to him. It was Neville Gorton of Coventry of whom William Temple said that he was a man through whom the Holy Spirit blew in great gusts. In a striking tribute to him in his book of memories, *A Shaft of Sunlight,* Philip Mason has written:

"I have never known anyone who was less a respecter of persons. His affection included

the most ignorant urchin at the bottom of the school

a shepherd he had met on the fells

the shoemaker behind his counter in the town

whoever in short he was talking to unless he showed himself callous or cruel or brutal. I never met him without feeling braced, invigorated, refreshed, aware that for a moment I had seen a tongue of flame".

How appropriately this might have been written about Joe Fison. He was christened Joseph Edward: his family called him Edward: his innumerable friends came to know him as Joe: the Scots in Aberdeen called him Atomic Fison and others substituted Nuclear Fison: and finally he became Joseph Sarum. But most remember him still as Joe and I have not hesitated therefore to use this name in writing about him.

I am deeply indebted to a number of friends who have supplied me with material. The Revd. Trevor Jones who wrote a long essay on Joe and received a number of letters about him has kindly allowed me to read both the essay and the letters. The Revd. Ian Thomson and Dr. Marcus Gregory who were intimately in touch with him over many years have generously shared with me some of their memories. I must also express my thanks to others who have supplied me with information about particular stages of his career.

I am above all grateful to Kathleen Fison, Joe's sister, who filed many of his letters, tabulated the main events of his life and supplied me with detailed information about his family background: and to Irene, his widow, who gave me free access to Joe's papers, answered so many of my questions, bore patiently with my hesitations and tried in every way possible to assist me in gaining a true perspective of what was certainly an unconventional life.

Finally I wish to express on my own behalf and on behalf of Joe's family and friends our profound appreciation of Lord Coggan's interest which prompted him to recommend publication and to write a foreword: and of the very generous grants made by the S.P.C.K. and by the Sarum St. Michael Educational Charity Trust which made publication possible. We are also greatly indebted to Mr. Robin Waterfield who has taken a keen personal interest in the production of the book by the Amate Press which he directs.

Oxford   F. W. Dillistone
1983

1

Fertilisers and Explosives

The last week-end of January 1966 was a landmark in the history of the Suffolk town of Stowmarket. A cluster of events — the opening of a new Hall, a historical lecture, an exhibition, a parade — marked the 25th. anniversary of the destruction of the Stowmarket Congregational Church on January 31st. 1941. A lone German raider, passing over the town, dropped a stick of bombs that shattered a number of homes in a quiet road and reduced the Congregational church to a ruined shell.

Erected in 1861, this church was an imposing Gothic building, planned to be the place of worship for a large and influential congregation. Among its staunchest supporters was the Prentice family and now, in the act of thanksgiving, designed as the climax of the restoration ceremonies, the preacher was the Right Rev. Joseph Edward Fison, Bishop of Salisbury, son of Ethel Prentice who had been a devoted member of the Church in her early years.

The Sermon began dramatically:

"I was brought up in two churches of entirely different outlook. When I was in my grandmother's home I worshipped here in a Church whose optimism was infectious. When I was in my own home, I worshipped in the Parish Church, whose pessimism was equally infectious.

"When I was in grandmother's home I heard many wonderful children's stories (none of which I remember!) and many sermons on the Sermon on the Mount — a lot about Jesus and perhaps not so much about God. When I was in my own home I heard many texts (none of which I remember except the one on the War Memorial which was not in the Bible!)

'When the power of the city shall seem great, will you consider then that it was purchased by valiant men and by men who knew their duty'. (Pericles) and I heard many sermons from St. Paul's Epistles and more about God than Jesus except that in every sermon the blood of Jesus was explicitly mentioned.

"When I was in my grandmother's home I heard here much about ethics and social reponsibility and saw much practical action (e.g. Boys' Brigade and the Camp at Walton-on-Naze.) When I was in my own home I heard much about doctrine and missionary and evangelistic work and attended many prayer meetings — we were (I remember) keener on Baffin Land than

1

on Boys' Brigade.

"When I was in my grandmother's home (if I had lived there more) I had human friendship and fellowship and could live in the 'world'. When I was in my own home I experienced more human loneliness and at the same time more fellowship with God and I had to live out of the 'world'.

"These profound (perhaps I exaggerate) differences had nothing to do with denomination at all. Even the way in which in my grandmother's home we recognized (or was it really true?) that the Church people looked down on the Chapel people could be matched by the way in which in my own home we imagined (or was it really true?) that the High Church people looked down on the Low church people. It was a great event if I went to the Parish Church in Stowmarket and it was quite a greater event if I went to the High Church in my own home''.

From this series of vivid contrasts the preacher chose one for special emphasis. It was the contrast between optimism, (which could easily appear 'shallow and cheap') and pessimism (which could easily appear 'grim and ghastly'). His own family had, he recalled, experienced what seemed to be an unmitigated disaster in 1871. The Congregational Church at Stowmarket had been completely wrecked in 1941. In each case the reaction could have been either a contrived escapism or an abject despair. Instead there was the Christian way of faith in God in face of all the contraries of human experience.

"In the world ye shall have tribulation; but be of good cheer, I have overcome the world''.

"This" the preacher declared "is no gospel of proximate optimism or ultimate pessimism. This is a doctrine of proximate pessimism encircled by ultimate optimism. This is the faith of the Cross and the Resurrection — not that the worst won't happen, but that even if it does it can be turned into something better than if it had never happened''.

When he preached this sermon, Joe Fison was in his sixtieth year. From his earliest days he had lived within contrasting situations: only for short periods had there ever been smooth and straightforward progress. Yet he had never complained. He feared stagnation and complacency more than anything else. *The Christian Hope,* the title of his most substantial book, became the watchword of his whole career. He began life between the staunch independency of East Anglian Congregationalism and the intense conservatism of low-Church Anglicanism. He ended between the unceasing institutional demands of a traditional English diocese and the even more insistent calls of an evangelistic and pastoral ministry.

II

In 1662, the Rev. John Fairfax, an ancestor of the Prentices, refused to take the oath of allegiance to King Charles II and was in consequence ejected from his living in Barking. With others, who had similarly refused the oath, he laid the foundations of dissent in Suffolk and from that time congregationalism flourished both in East Anglia and in New England to which 'better land' so many frustrated pilgrims emigrated. One of the most distinguished pastors from the Stowmarket district became minister of the famous Old South Church in Boston, a place of meeting for conspirators at the time of the American Revolution.

The Prentices were for generations landowners and businessmen. Ethel Prentice's father, Mr. Edward Henry Prentice, was a director in the firm of the Patent Safety Guncotton Company of which the Chairman and General Director were also Prentices. Over a long period the manufacture of guncotton in Europe had been a hazardous process but an invention in 1865 seemed to guarantee safety and the business prospects for the Stowmarket firm were bright. Then came disaster. In August 1871 an unusual spell of hot weather caused the cartridges in the three magazines to explode, leaving a chasm 10 feet deep and 100 feet across.

Edward Prentice, together with William Prentice, his nephew, drove at once to the works which had been completely wrecked. Courageously, but ill-advisedly, they both went inside to draw boxes of cartridges away from the flames and a further explosion killed them instantly. Edward's widow was left with two daughters, Minnie aged three and Ethel aged one, while a third daughter, Connie, was born after the tragic death of her father. These proved to be a remarkable trio, who in course of time dedicated themselves to the activities of the Chapel to which their mother belonged.

For more than two centuries the social life of Suffolk had remained remarkably stable, even though a succession of families made their way across the Atlantic. There were Dennys and Southgates, there were Prentices and Fisons, and in the middle of the 18th. century a Fison married a Prentice. There was yet another intermarriage between the two families before, in 1903, Frederick Flint Fison married Ethel Prentice (Frederick's mother's maiden name was Flint). Thus in Eastern Suffolk Fison-Prentice links extended over many years and whereas the name Fison has gained world fame because of fertilisers, the Prentice name might have become equally famous had it been common knowledge that Prentices were amongst the founders of the firm which ultimately became I.C.I.

Joe Fison's forbears then were Suffolk yeomen, tanners, maltsters, bakers, manufacturers of chemical products. The Fisons were loyal members of the Church of England and generally conservative in outlook. The Prentices were radical in politics and dissenters in religion. All were god-fearing and Bible-loving and gave of their services gladly in church and chapel. There was a new development however in the social life of both families when Frederick, after a distinguished career in the Queen Elizabeth School, Ipswich, gained a leaving exhibition to Oxford. Having entered St. John's College in 1895 to read mathematics, he gained a first-class in Mathematical Moderations.

While at St. John's he excelled as an all-round athlete. He played football and tennis for the College and rowed two years in one of the College boats. In addition he became an ardent cyclist and regularly, at beginning and end of term, rode the 88 miles between home and college. Though his performance in Maths Finals was disappointing, his tutor regarded him as a good scholar and he decided to make teaching his career. After a short period in Lancashire, he was appointed Senior Mathematical Master at Hereford Cathedral School and there he settled happily in 1901.

Meanwhile he remained loyal to his home-ties in Suffolk and in 1903 Ethel Prentice became his wife. In spite of the earlier links between the two families, it appears that the marriage was not altogether approved of by their elders: their son, Joseph Edward, who was born in 1906, became aware at an early age of a certain tension between the two sides of his family background. It was far from easy for the young bride to take up residence in a West Country. Cathedral Close, possibly one of the most conservative in the country. She found herself unaccustomed to the traditional patterns of social behaviour and although she was an occasional communicant in the Church of England, she was not confirmed until many years later.

However, life at Hereford proved to be generally happy, especially when, soon after their marriage, she and her husband took charge of the school's new boarding-house. She became devoted to the six boys under her care and for recreation went long journeys on a tandem cycle with her enthusiastic partner. When in March 1906 her son was born, there seemed every prospect of a settled period in the school with full opportunity for the raising of her own family.

Almost immediately, alas, a shadow fell across the family's fortunes. T.B. was still at that time a dreaded enemy and, in spite of his fine athletic background, Frederick Fison began to show symptoms of the disease. From 1907 when he left Hereford, until 1919 when he died at Clevedon in Somerset, his career was punctuated by changes of location, by ups and downs of his illness and by anxieties about teaching-posts. He taught for short periods at Repton, at the Royal Naval College, Osborne and at King Edward VII Grammar School, King's Lynn. He even applied for a head-mastership and his testimonials show how highly he was regarded as a teacher. But in 1912 T.B. set in badly and after that it was a question of going from one seaside resort to another without finding any permanent cure.

III

The bond between Joe and his father proved to be particularly close. The growing boy found himself in a family circle which might have been dominated by feminine interests. His grandmother Prentice, herself a widow, was a tiny erect figure with a resolute spirit, devoted to her family. His mother's two sisters, neither of whom married, were unceasingly active in all kinds of religious and artistic concerns — organ and piano playing, choral singing, painting, photography, and Sunday-school teaching. His mother inevitably assumed a certain leadership in family affairs because of her husband's physical limitations and the one other close member of the circle was a younger sister born in 1908. Joe's father did his utmost to share his son's interests and set him on the way to attain a more than average proficiency in ball-games: golf, fives, cricket, and tennis especially. They walked together and Joe learned about maps and foreign travel.

As far as religious faith and practice were concerned, father and mother, though brought up in differing church traditions, were at one in their acknowledgement of the authority of the Bible and in their commitment to the discipline of prayer. Evangelical Anglicanism and Puritan Dissent laid equal emphases on regular Bible study, on intercessory prayer and on service to the community.

Joe's father was by nature buoyant and friendly, though of a serious disposition, a popular figure in school and college, partly by reason of his proficiency in games. He was himself a teetotaler but did not attempt to impose this restriction on his friends. He was an exellent teacher, easily maintaining discipline and inspiring enthusiasm both in the classroom and on the playing field. To devote his energies to the care of the boys under his charge was his particular form of Christian service.

By contrast, his mother was lively, outgoing, sometimes impulsive, deeply affectionate. She was athletic and something of a tomboy. Throughout her life children and young people would listen to and confide in her, feeling in her presence a kind of gentle strength. She wrote poems, and in them revealed something of her own character:-

"I climb because I must"

"That urge that comes from God

And moves men to the goal".

"I should like to go down as a fighter!...

To endure to the end, and to follow

Wherever the leading may be!".

After the onset of the T.B. in 1907, the Fison family occupied temporary homes until, in 1909, a house was bought at Hunstanton and links were renewed with the East Coast. This enabled Joe's father to accept the appointment at King's Lynn to which he went to and fro every day by bicycle. (He was, however, persuaded to attach the recently invented auto-cycle). But this lasted for only 2 years and then came a succession of visits to warmer areas in Devon and Somerset. Finally, after his death, a family home was established in a cottage at Felixstowe and there Joe spent his holidays from boarding school and College. In these holdays he was back in Fison and Prentice country, maintaining a Fison loyalty by attending the local Church of England but in other ways surrounded by the traditions and activities of the Prentice clan. Joe partnered his mother at tennis in Tournament Mixed Doubles and played golf with his aunt on the Stowmarket Course. In this clan, sport, art and Christian service, in ascending order, were the dominant concerns.

IV

With the father's illness necessitating a constant change of climate, the problem of school-attendance for the growing boy became urgent. His father gave whatever assistance he could though Joe was no mathematician. Boarding school seemed the obvious solution and in 1917 he was sent to Orley Farm Preparatory School in Harrow. However he was not entirely deprived of a home atmosphere for he boarded with the Ridsdale family at the Roxeth Vicarage. There he was to remain until, having gained an entrance scholarship to Shrewsbury, by virtue of an outstanding English paper and proficiency in Latin, he entered that School in 1920.

His life at Orley Farm and Roxeth Vicarage seems to have been pleasant enough. He gradually improved his position in Class, gaining his best marks in English and Latin and beginning to learn Greek. The letters to his parents tell proudly of his successes on the cricket field; his leisure reading was particularly directed to military history and to developments in the war which was in progress at the beginning of his residence in Harrow. The Christmas holidays in 1918-19 took him to Clevedon where his parents and sister were staying and on January 14th. near the time for returning to school, his father died of pleurisy and pericarditis.

It is impossible to gauge the deep psychological effect on a boy less then 13 years old of the death of a father who had been a companion, a teacher, a hero in the world of sport and yet also an object of pity and concern because of the constant recurrence of physical weakness. It was a traumatic experience. Yet back at school he was soon caught up in the struggle for marks and victory at games which characterised its normal life. But when holidays came there was no longer the male presence and Joe was surrounded by motherly care, either at his grandmother's home in Stowmarket or in the Felixstowe cottage.

The church tradition at Roxeth was evangelical and so comparable to that of his home surroundings. To learn and follow the Christian way of life by the aid of a growing knowledge of the Bible was the ideal set before him and this he seems to have accepted without serious question. St. Andrew's Church at Felixstowe was a centre of evangelistic activity, supporting the Convention and the Seaside Mission which were annual features of the town. Joe had no dramatic conversion. He identified himself with the activities which his family supported, showing already that gay enthusiasm which proved so attractive to young people in particular. When he came home for the holidays there were peals of laughter as he gathered a group of friends around him either for sport or for some enterprise connected with the Church. A friend who lived in Stowmarket and often saw him when he visited his grandmother remembers him as 'very good to look at', 'always full of bright ideas', never partronising to his younger friends who assisted him in his practical jokes, already displaying that enthusiastic energy which characterised him through out his life. Already there was a feeling that a career of distinction lay ahead of him.

2

Classics and the Bible

At Orley Farm Preparatory School Joe gained a firm grounding in Latin and his performance in the Shrewsbury Scholarship Examination was good enough to gain him a place amongst the classical scholars. He began to learn Greek and during five years at Shrewsbury and four at Oxford his academic studies were devoted almost entirely to classical languages and literature.

Shrewsbury he took in his stride. There seem to have been no major crises nor was he unhappy in public school life. He seemed to possess a natural cheerfulness which enabled him to make satisfactory progress with his work and to play games with enthusiasm. The classics masters did not regard him as outstanding in his prose compositions but otherwise had few complaints. He was a sound cricketer, represented the School in the Fives Pair against Eton and in the holidays became an excellent tennis player.

Obviously the authorities trusted him even if his conduct was at times too much that of a professional humourist and he became first a house monitor and then a school prepositor. There was perhaps some uncertainty about his prospects for an Oxford scholarship because of his weakness in Latin composition but as it turned out he gained the top classics award at Queen's in December 1924 and went into residence there the following October. According to normal practice he was thus set to read Mods and Greats during the coming four years.

All this time he was exposed to various religious influences though it is impossible to estimate which were the most powerful. As his Stowmarket sermon shows, his grandmother was a staunch Congregationalist, holding that the Bible provided the necessary standards of behaviour for individual and social life. To live according to its precepts was the whole duty of man. His mother could be described as a reluctant Anglican, loyal to her husband and the Church to which he belonged, but uneasy with its emphasis on sacramental ordinances. She requested that Joe should not be confirmed before he was 16 years of age and she herself postponed receiving confirmation until some time after her husband's death. In any case the Church of England in which she, and her children when at home, worshipped was strongly protestant.

But during many months of each year Joe regularly attended

services away from home. At Roxeth the influence would have been comparable to that of his mother's church but at Shrewsbury the chapel services would have been attended as part of the corporate school routine rather than as a voluntary means of spiritual edification. Joe's letters home included an occasional reference to a sermon in chapel: one by the gloomy Dean (Inge), one by the Headmaster of Eton who surprised the boys by declaring that Christ would probably have been a supporter of Labour: but if there was any influence through chapel services it must have been largely unconscious.

However there was one other influence which undoubtedly left its mark on him. Several of the East Coast seaside resorts had become favourite centres for the August activities of the Children's Special Service Mission and two of these were Hunstanton and Felixstowe. When at home for the summer holidays, therefore, Joe shared quite naturally in the beach services. His buoyancy was infectious and he seems to have had no inhibitions about his Christian commitment and confession. An open-air, unconventional expression of Christian faith was already making its appeal to him and through him.

II

To public-school boys who, in the early 1920's were still subject to a quite rigid discipline, life at Oxford or Cambridge brought an immense sense of emancipation. Yet the sudden absence of all but a few rules also brought its challenge. Was it worth-while to attend lectures? What amount of work was necessary to satisfy one's tutor? How could one choose between the multifarious interests competing for one's attention?

Joe could give full rein to his enthusiasm for sports. He played some rugby and cricket at Queen's but tennis was his first love. He practised in his room on the wood panelling and ultimately became captain of the College VI. Had it not been for trouble with the cartilage of his knee he might have gained still higher distinction.

About his academic work he made little reference in his letters and in later life he affirmed that he was not really a classical scholar. Though he entered Queen's with the highest award of his year, he failed to gain a First Class either in Honour Moderations (the real proof of proficiency in ancient languages) or in Greats (the test of knowledge of ancient history and of the handling of philosophical problems). There is no evidence that this was due to lack of application. It seems rather that the great tradition, stemming from Greece and Rome, never captured his whole-hearted interest. Careful examination of linguistic details, rigorous discussion of logical problems did not belong to his mental make-up. He did his assigned work satisfactorily but it lacked the touch of inspiration and the over-all grasp of the subject which would have given him a first class. That was to be gained in a different field.

Of the many other activities which might have captured his interest and allegiance, none occupied so large a place in his university career as did the various forms of Christian fellowship and witness in which he was involved. In Oxford at the time there were the College Chapels and certain churches, Anglican and Nonconformist, which maintained regular services and promoted varieties of pastoral care for students. In addition there were three major religious societies, each representing a particular slant or emphasis. The Oxford University Church Union was Anglo Catholic in its outlook and promoted liturgical interests. The Student Christian Movement was interdenominational and liberal in its outlook and promoted social interests. The third society had been established after the War to represent evangelicalism and had taken as its name the Oxford University Bible Union. But in the spring of 1925 a majority voted to drop this name and, while still retaining a measure of independence, to become the Devotional Union of the Student Christian Movement. For Joe it was natural that, with his own evangelical background, he should throw in his lot with the D.U.

For the time being the programme of activities carried on by the D.U. continued much as before. There was a weekly meeting addressed by an invited speaker, a daily prayer meeting and an open-air service on Sunday evenings at the Martyrs' Memorial. In addition personal evangelism was encouraged and each year parties were organised to attend the Keswick Convention and to assist in one or other of the summer missions of the Children's Special Service Mission.

Joe quickly identified himself with this group and in so doing, as his letters to his mother and grandmother show, adopted a pattern of religious activity which won their full approval. He named various figures, well known in evangelical circles, who had visited Oxford and he told of the inspiring talks they had given. Not that he confined himself to listening only to those who were considered 'sound' on matters relating to the Bible. He gave generous assessments of those whose theological stance might seem open to question. But there was no doubt about what kind of speaker gained his enthusiastic reponse. The evangelist, the missionary, the pioneer who faced danger as he bore faithful witness to Christ — these were the men of fire who warmed his heart.

Such men. however, did not naturally belong to the circles of recognised Church leaders nor to the large interdenominational organisations such as the Student Christian Movement or the Y.M.C.A. The S.C.M. fostered radical thinking about social and political issues such as poverty, racism, class-conflicts and economic inequalities. Evangelicals, whether in strong student bodies such as the C.I.C.C.U. at Cambridge or in voluntary evangelistic organisations centred in London made it their aim to proclaim the Gospel in its simplicity so that individuals might hear and be converted. The constantly recurring question was whether it was possible for Evangelicals to share in the wider intellectual and social concerns and at the same time preserve their 'cutting edge', a clear-cut witness and commitment to the saving work of Christ.

At Oxford and Cambridge the question was often made more complex by conflicts of loyalties. Men and women came to the University from strong Evangelical backgrounds — family or school or denomination. Their parents might have been missionaries in such a society as the China Inland Mission with its firm Biblical basis and its evangelistic zeal. Or the denominational allegiance might have been to the Plymouth Brethren or to conservative Baptists. To become members of an Oxford society whose basis conformed to family traditions seemed a way of furthering already existing convictions and commitments. But could they be preserved when intimately associated with a large amorphous organisation whose main purpose was to study and discuss wide-open questions about the nature of Christianity and its relation to world-problems?

As I have noted, Joe came to Oxford just at the time when the decision in favour of such an association had been made. A few, however, though accepting the decision, remained unhappy about it and many of their acquaintances outside Oxford deplored it. Joe was never intolerant nor did he ever try to withdraw into a ghetto. He was outgoing, buoyant, phenomenally quick to see the funny side of things and to explode in some witty remark at which no one could take offence. Yet he was troubled about the situation. In his third year, when he had to find lodgings out of College, he shared rooms in Divinity Road with a friend who was dedicated to medical missionary service and who felt strongly that the Union committed to Biblical doctrine and evangelistic witness ought to preserve an independent existence. At length Joe himself came to the conclusion that separation was inevitable and he thus became one of the founder members of the Society which

11

adopted a pre-war name and became known as the Oxford Inter-Collegiate Christian Union.

III

All this time Joe could hardly give his mind to exploring the intellectual problems of the Christian faith in any depth. He was under constant pressure to produce essays on the history and philosophy of the classical world. His reading of the Bible and of Christian literature was directed to devotional needs and to evangelistic aims. His responsibility, he believed, was to listen to the word of God and to proclaim it. He could speak vividly and vigorously. His stentorian efforts in the open-air at the Martyrs' Memorial gained him lasting fame. It was said that his voice could be heard all the way to St. Giles's Church. And he did this without fear or favour, simply trying to relate the Gospel to the basic needs of human hearts.

As the time for Finals approached, however, the question of what next was bound to arise. Should he seek ordination? Or should he prepare himself for foreign missionary service? For the moment no decision was made on these ultimate questions. Instead he decided to read the Honour School of Theology in his fifth year and to do this while residing at Wycliffe Hall. If finally the call to ordination became clear, the year spent at a Theological College would be regarded as part of the necessary preparation.

Joe came to the Hall as a keen member of the O.I.C.C.U. and continued to join in its devotional and evangelistic activities. But to read Theology in one year was a big assignment to which he needed to give maximum attention. Yet he came to the study of theology with a sense of release. As I have already suggested, he was never fully at home in the classical world, never in his element. When it came to the Biblical world, however, the fire began to burn. He already knew the text intimately, having, like the young Timothy, inherited a love of Scripture both from his mother and his grandmother. He was equipped to deal with linguistic requirements in Latin and Greek. And his training in Greats had sharpened his critical faculties, enabling him to tackle complex historical problems with resolution and good judgment.

Joe was fortunate to have as his tutor the Rev. J. P. Thornton-Duesbury who had himself read Mods, Greats and Theology just four years earlier. This is his memory of working with Joe in the academic year 1929-30:

"I was lucky enough to have as good a pair of pupils as a

Tutor could ever have, though I took them singly — Joe and H. E. W. Turner who recently retired from the Senior Theology Chair at Durham. I think 'Hughie' knew more theology than I did even then, as his essays usually took 45 minutes to read! But Joe was the most fascinating and enjoyable pupil I ever had. Personally he was the liveliest and most attractive young man you could meet; intellectually he not only had a first-class mind of a particularly quick and sensitive character, but he was just emerging from the rather rigid Conservative Evangelical background in which he had been brought up. I had myself been through a somewhat similar, though much less traumatic experience, and my job as tutor was really to act as midwife at the birth of the new Joe! It was not a Caesarean operation or a breech delivery. It came perfectly naturally, though childbirth is always a bit painful, as babies find leaving the security of the womb! My part was just to be *there* — to listen or let Joe talk his way into the wider perspective of the faith. I don't *think* (tho' I may be wrong here) he ever lost the deep conviction of faith in Christ or went through agonies of doubt or dereliction but it must have been a costly process anyhow as doubtless it cost him the loss of some of his earlier friends''.

This account is most illuminating in regard to Joe's development intellectually during the year in question but I doubt whether a new Joe had as yet quite established his own identity. The Honours School of Theology demanded a detailed knowledge of the Biblical text, a thorough acquaintance with the historical and documentary problems which a study of the text is bound to involve, and a mastery of the history of the Church in the first four centuries of its life with special reference to certain patristic texts. Joe grappled with all this enthusiastically and it was a notable day for Wycliffe Hall when the examiners placed its two members named by Mr. Thornton-Duesbury in the First Class. The Principal's steady advocacy of an honest wrestling with the intellectual problems which Christians should face was beginning to be vindicated. But Joe was not yet entirely 'out of the womb'.

3

'Breaking the Custom'

In 1930 Joe was 24 years old. He could have proceeded at once to ordination but he was not yet convinced that this was to be his ultimate vocation. He had come to know and admire laymen who were dedicating their lives to pioneer missionary work, preaching the Gospel in areas where no organised Church life existed. He had no doubts about his call to be a witness for Christ. But how exactly this was to be done had not yet become clear.

Moreover, there were certain unresolved tensions in his life which could perhaps only be eased by 'distancing', by withdrawing for a while from his immediate associations of home on the one side and the place of education on the other. Over a period of 13 years his life had been geared to a regular rhythm: Stowmarket and (from 1921 onwards) Felixstowe in vacations, school or college in term-time. The former environment was dominantly feminine and biblical: the latter dominantly masculine and classical. Oxford had seemed to establish a more unified pattern religiously but even there, towards the end of the period in question, the possibility of breaking with past loyalties had begun to appear.

There are too many uncertainties in psychological theorizing to allow one to speak confidently about the effect on Joe's development of the almost complete absence of male influences in his home environment. First his grandmother had been widowed at an early age and left with three small daughters. Of these only one, Joe's mother, married and she too lost her husband when her son and daughter had not yet reached adolescence. This meant that from the age of 13 onwards Joe was surrounded, when at home in Suffolk, by grandmother, mother, aunts and sister, all devoted to him and looking on him as the future man of the family. He in turn was devoted to them all and aware of a major responsibility towards his mother and sister. It was an attractive family circle, its members talented, comfortably off financially, full of good works and church activities, enjoying travel and play.

But while he remained in the midst of such an often adoring community could he attain his own full independent manhood? While away at school and college he could make many male friends and find satisfaction in many male activities — sport in particular. Yet was he going to be able to branch out on his own, to found a family of his own? Probably in 1930 such questions were hardly conscious but there is sufficient evidence to show that towards the end of the 30's they were very much in his mind. How far had he really attained freedom?

Another aspect of his dependence upon the East Anglian family background was that of his understanding of the Christian faith. Whatever differences there may have been between Congregationalism and evangelical Anglicanism in Suffolk, in both communities Holy Scripture was the all-important rule for faith and conduct. Joe's mother, as he declared in one of his books, had taught him to love the Old Testament. Preachers and seaside missioners upheld the authority of the Bible: questions raised by methods of historical and literary criticism were either not mentioned or dismissed as detrimental to faith. Could Joe remain loyal to Christianity as believed and practised by those he so much respected and loved and at the same time be ruthlessly honest in his attitude to the Scriptures?

Perhaps his departure for a while from England at least helped to settle the second problem. He decided that after his year at Wycliffe Hall he would accept appointment to the English Mission College in Cairo and it was there that in a quite dramatic way release suddenly came.

"I was in the small hall of the English Mission College. A Maltese boy named Nestor Cardullo came up to me and asked the question 'do you believe the whole bible is true from Genesis to Revelation?' It was no time for quibbling: it was a genuine question and demanded a genuine answer. I gave it and replied 'Yes' and, as I said it, I knew for the first time that it was a lie and that I did not so believe it. That incident marked the end of eight or ten years of what I believed were fundamentalist convictions. During those years I had worked with the C.S.S.M. and had been one of the refounders of the O.I.C.C.U. And I had had the privilege of working in the C.M.J. (Church Mission to Jews) Cairo Mission and of visiting Abyssinia with that great pioneer missionary . . . Alfred Buxton. All that time the basic presuppositions of biblical fundamentalism had underlain what I believed to be my religious convictions. On that 1933 morning in Cairo I did not change my views, but I suddenly discovered what my views were or, perhaps better, were not.

"Now to me that was something, I suppose, in a very small way of what Berdyaev describes as the liberation of a man who comes out of a religion of bondage into a religion of freedom. And, as he says, for such a pilgrim the idea of going back is unthinkable. One point alone stood clear as a result of that experience. No longer had all truth to be submitted to the bible and forced to conform to it: no longer had the bible itself to be accepted as infallible . . . All critical conclusions might be wrong in every particular point. But the critical approach was vindicated. That was the liberating truth that then gripped me. And it remains as fundamental to me to-day as it appeared fifteen years ago.

"Yet before that Maltese boy put that question to me, I neither knew what I really believed (though I thought I did) nor could I imagine how faith in Christ could long survive without faith in the infallible book. As I interpret my own past, it seems not unfair to describe my worship before 1933 as in part at least idolatrous . . . and the idolatry is none the less deadly for being enshrined in so comparatively spiritual a form. The explicit emergence of this biblical and fundamentalist idolatry as a theological phenomenon of the last one hundred and fifty years of evangelical protestantism is to be distinguished from the simple biblical faith of Christian people all down the ages. It is an understandable, even if regrettable, reaction to the rise of biblical critical thought and it only assumes an idolatrous form when it makes an explicit dogma out of an implicit attitude. That it has become a twentieth-century idolatry I have no doubt whatever. And its popularity and pragmatic evangelistic value is only proof of the incurably idolatrous tendency of the human heart''.

(The Blessing of the Holy Spirit 151f)

II

In the light of this vividly expressed apologia it is hardly possible to accept all the implications of Mr. Thornton-Duesbury's analogy. The year at Wycliffe did not bring about a complete delivery (or deliverance) nor was a totally new Joe born. According to his own testimony, what it really did was to undermine an attitude to the Bible inherited and outwardly accepted as true. His mind considered the arguments of biblical scholars critically yet he tried to persuade himself that his own dogma of biblical infallibility was still secure. Then suddenly a direct question caused this dogma to collapse like a house of cards. He realised now that what had seemed to be a tower of strength had in reality been a prison. He could continue to cherish the Bible and to draw from it unlimited inspiration through the guidance of the Spirit. Yet it need no longer be hedged about by such a term as *infallible.* From this time onward he was able to proclaim a gospel of religious freedom in a way that he had never known before.

Still this proved to be far from easy. He loved his family and his Oxford friends and he hated to hurt any of them. Moreover his heart was altogether convenanted to friends like Alfred Buxton who risked life and limb in the service of the Gospel and won the allegiance of the most primitive of peoples by the sheer outpouring of themselves in compassionate care. Not long after the experience with the Maltese boy, Joe decided to return to England and to Oxford in particular and his new freedom had in fact to stand the strain of being the object of mistrust and misunderstanding in certain quarters.

I have jumped ahead to recount the critical incident in Cairo because of its importance in Joe's search for freedom. But something must be said about his work in Cairo and about his pilgrimage to Abyssinia in one of the school vacations.

During his years in Oxford, whether at Queen's or at Wycliffe Hall, he had allied himself fully with Christians or whatever denomination who were fired with evangelistic and missionary zeal. Though he retained his Anglican allegiance and, in 1929-30, carried on theological studies while residing at Wycliffe Hall, he had no conviction of being called to ordination. The far strong urge was to commit himself to some kind of pioneer missionary work overseas and this could perfectly well be carried on as a layman.

The English Mission College was founded in 1924, the first Protestant day-school to be established in Cairo. It started in a somewhat dilapidated building in the older part of the city, initially for girls only. But numbers grew rapidly and in 1926 a boys' section was added. By 1930, when Joe went out, there were already some 30 members of the Staff (some part-time) and nearly 30 different nationalities were represented amongst the boys and girls. Lessons and games were organised very much according to an English pattern and time was allotted within the school routine for Christian prayers and Bible instruction.

Joe was exceedingly fond of and popular with children and had found no difficulty in capturing their interest in Sunday Schools and seaside missions in England. But to be responsible for regular teaching and discipline in a multi-racial school in an unfamilar environment with often trying climatic conditions was quite a different matter. The boys came from homes with no traditions of behaviour comparable to those still largely observed in England. Joe's innate sense of fun was such that he often found their schemes and devices very amusing but he knew that if he once lost control, any attempts to teach would have little chance of success. Although the boys' school was not

17

large — about 120 boys — he often found himself with a class of 30 to keep in order. A further duty, which was partly pleasurable but often exhausting, was that of taking charge of Physical Exercise at the end of each afternoon from Monday to Friday. Out in the playground it was relatively easy for the boys to get up to all kinds of tricks and Joe's resources were stretched to the limit.

As the College was a day-school, the weekends gave opportunities for exploring Cairo and its neighbourhood. The English military presence was still prominent and there were a good many English residents. On Sundays there were regular services and Sunday School at the College and in these Joe played a full part. He maintained a steady programme of reading, eagerly welcoming newspapers and periodicals from England; in books he showed a particular penchant for biography, his imagination being stimulated by records of heroes of faith and adventure, and it could be inferred that his own future commitment was likely to be in this direction. To this end his all-important vacation was that arranged for the summer of 1932 when, through the financial assistance of his family, he was able to spend two months in Abyssinia. This experience proved to be in some respects a turning-point in the development of his own understanding of the nature of his future ministry.

III

On July 12, 1932, he set sail from Alexandria to Djibouti. He found that many of his fellow passengers were en route for Madagascar and this brought a challenge to launch out into some quite lengthy conversations in French. He found opportunities for distributing literature and had the satisfaction of knowing that one Malagasy, in response, read nearly the whole of St. Matthew's gospel. Normally only two trains ran weekly from Djibouti to Abyssinia but Joe and his friend Alfred Buxton, who had come to the port by boat from Mombasa, were fortunate in finding a special train returning to Addis Ababa after bringing down one of the royal family to the coast.

As the train climbed up towards the mountainous regions, they gained some relief from the heat but this was offset by an abundance of rain. Indeed the two months he spent in Abyssinia seem to have been punctuated by a succession of violent thunderstorms, and the weather was so wet that any hope of seeing much of the country outside Addis Ababa vanished. However he and his companion were welcomed with characteristic American hospitality into the home of Dr.

Lambie and his wife who were in charge of the work of the Sudan Interior Mission.

Behind the visit there lay a definite objective: the Bible Churchmen's Missionary Society in England, seeking possible new areas for its work, had commissioned Alfred Buxton, who was then working in Kenya, to spy out the land, as it were, and report. Already the S.I.M. was well-established and, in addition, the Seventh Day Adventists were making their own particular witness. There was a Swedish Mission, while a church in Addis Ababa, served by an S.P.G. chaplain, catered for English residents. By far the largest representative of the Christian faith, however, was the ancient church of Ethiopia. The justification for any possible Anglican presence was first the fact that there were certain areas in the country which were still largely pagan and then that the indigenous Church had been for centuries virtually isolated from contacts with the rest of Christendom.

On arrival Joe and Alfred were invited at once to share in a convention of missionaries and their people for the deepening of spiritual life, an excellent opportunity for learning about the kind of missionary opportunities that were actually available. In addition there were meetings to which members of local churches, Ethiopian, Armenian and Greek had been invited and to which the response had been encouraging.

With little hope of trekking out to other areas, Joe set to work to gain some knowledge of Amharic for he was convinced that this was the first requirement if he were ever to return as a full-time missionary. He found an excellent teacher in the Swedish Mission and went to and fro on a borrowed mule for his daily instruction. In a letter he explained: "I am learning the language (a) because I don't want to be idle (b) because very few missionaries here know it at all well (c) because I think it is possible that I may be meant to return here later on, though how or in what connection I haven't the slightest idea (d) because I vaguely have in mind the future possibility of learning Geez and then I could produce my B.D. thesis without much difficulty. I should think, though, the value of the same, apart from my personal swollen head, might be problematical". After referring to a 'severe lesson' that morning in Amharic verbs, he switched to a charming picture of Wandimo 'whom I dearly love,' 2½ years old, one of the children of the house-servant, recently shorn of her former hair-style and only retaining 'a short forest just on the crown'.

So the days went by. There were visits to the American and British Legations, a trip out to the Leper Hospital and opportunities to learn about some of the fasts and festivals of the Ethiopian Church. One of these which Joe described at length, was the ushering in of the new year at St. George's Cathedral early in September. As the Ethiopian calendar works on a four year cycle, named after the four evangelists, 1932 was the occasion for discharging John and welcoming Matthew. There was chanting in Geez, rattling of little silver cymbals, grinding of prayer sticks on the floor and dancing. In the Mass that followed, the priest and the young deacons were often behind the screen in the Holy of Holies. Wearing beautifully coloured velvet cloaks and caps, the deacons read lections and led the chanting before bringing out bread and wine which they gave first to the men and then to women who were segregated round a corner. The worshippers were in church from 3 a.m. to 7.30 a.m. and, as Joe remarked, when he and his companions finally stepped out into the sunshine, it was like coming out of the time of David into the 20th. century.

Another interesting encounter, this one to lead to remarkable consequences, was his meeting with a young Coptic priest who at the time was acting as Chaplain to the Archbishop and who had started preaching services and Sunday-schools in the Ethiopian church. When a year or two later he wished to study in Britain, and learned that Joe was teaching in Oxford, he wrote to ask his help. So began a partnership and friendship which ripened while Marcus took his doctorate in Oxford, which continued in Egypt and Palestine during the war years and was ultimately sealed when Marcus was practising as a psychotherapist in London while Joe was in Salisbury. It was a creative friendship in which the doctor and the pastor were able to help one another in many different ways.

IV

What can be said about the effects of the Abyssinian visit on Joe's future? It is clear that his imagination had been fired by the possibility of doing evangelistic work in that country, not in opposition to the Ethiopian church but as helping it to become aware of its responsibilities towards the unevangelised tribes in the remoter parts of the land. He now saw the need more clearly but he also became more conscious of the practical difficulties. Near the end of his stay he wrote: "It's been a real blessing to me — though I know that's no good unless it's worked out practically. I know Alfred is impetuous and see it constantly. However I (a) am possessed of a mind and will (even if weak!) and (b) am trusting God for guidance. I do not suppose I shall altogether agree with him in his report but I quite think things may work out for me to return sometime somehow''. He had no doubt that he ought to return to the school in Cairo for another year but beyond that all was uncertain.

''I have no hesitation in going back (to Cairo)'', he wrote, ''So fear for me if you like (evidently his mother had been expressing anxiety about a possible commitment to a very uncertain missionary career) but do a little believing in God! As to Stowe and Oxford (evidently the Vicar of Mrs. Fison's home parish had been making suggestions about possible niches which Joe might fill) I know perfectly well that God has not called me to either of these places yet and frankly I doubt if He will. But I'm quite ready to return to England if He does. You may find, as I certainly found, real inspiration in noticing the development of Christ's character as a pattern for us in Luke 2. 40-end. In 40 'child' means literally 'little baby boy' and the law of his growth is in verse 42, 'after the custom'. In 43 'the child Jesus' should read 'the boy Jesus' and he became that by breaking the custom in virtue of the higher law of verse 49. And that leads on to the final 'Jesus' of 52 — the fully developed character — attained by the subjection of verse 51. That was a real flash of light for a talk last Sunday week and though I certainly couldn't claim to have reached the second stage, yet we must not be afraid of 'breaking the custom' if necessary — and perhaps some people at home and abroad don't quite grip that''.

I have quoted this passage from his letter in full because I believe it throws a good deal of light on Joe's own development. He was a man of extraordinarily affectionate nature. He loved his friends and they loved him. But in this flash of revelation — the Lucan passage seems to have made its full impact for the first time — he saw that it was essential at times to *break the custom*, whether that custom were familial or ecclesiastical or intellectual. Few who heard him speak in later years will forget his cry often repeated — 'He could only do his Father's will by breaking his mother's heart'. The reference to the Lucan passage seems obvious. ''I must be about my Father's business'' even if it means breaking bonds which at one stage of development have been of inestimable value. It was characteristic of Joe that, at any time, his innermost being could be pierced by some passage of Scripture and then his constant aim was to be obedient to the heavenly vision at whatever cost. He could scarcely have realised in Addis Ababa that 'breaking the custom' would soon lead him, down in Cairo, to break loose from the dogma of Biblical infallibility. It would be more than ten years before he achieved another freedom of a more personal kind.

Meanwhile he said good-bye to his friends, the Lambies, and then in Djibouti to Alfred Buxton who was returning to Kenya. The boat journey back was uneventful until he reached Suez where he disembarked in order to reach Cairo in time for the opening of the new term. He bargained with a taxi-driver who raced across the desert without adequate head-lights, dealt with a punctured tyre in Heliopolis and deposited Joe at the Mission College at about 1 a.m. His last year at the school was a decisive one in varying ways. I have already referred to the dramatic self-revelation which came about as a result of the question asked by a Maltese boy. Equally far-reaching was the decision he made to return to Oxford in order to join the Staff at Wycliffe Hall.

V

Joe had a boundless admiration for men like Alfred Buxton and for some of the missionaries he met in Addis Ababa, men who were fearless in face of danger and completely committed to the preaching of the gospel in lands where Christ was not already known. Yet, as he expressed it, he was possessed of *a mind.* It was a well-trained mind and he would not allow himself to be swept off his feet by any kind of mindless emotion. While in Addis Ababa, a well-known Canadian evangelist came to conduct meetings. In some respects his addresses were impressive. But Joe was puzzled by his appeal to his hearers' emotions and by his ideas on 'sanctification and kindred topics' which were more clear-cut than can be the case in most actual experiences. Particularly on the matter of guidance he could not believe that this depended simply upon flashes of inspiration coming to a lone individual. The mind had a part to play in weighing up pros and cons. A man must seek the advice of trusted advisers and be ruthlessly honest in regard to motives and relationships.

In February 1933 he began to consider his future in the light of an invitation received from the Principal of Wycliffe Hall. To his mother he confessed that if a suitable proposal were to come from Abyssinia ''I should jump at it'' but he was very sceptical about the practicability of new work in that country by an Anglican missionary society. He wondered if anything could be done in Jerusalem amongst members of the Ethiopian Church located there but that did not seem very likely. The prospect of theological teaching at Wycliffe attracted him, especially perhaps as he had been given more opportunities to teach scripture to senior boys in the Mission College and had found them exceedingly responsive to his attempts to grapple with such themes as the authority of the Bible and the place of reason in religion. But the position at Wycliffe would involve ordination and that, he saw clearly, meant a decision affecting his whole future. "Ordination is a distinctly irrevocable step". Was this the way forward into a life-vocation? "But for that I think I'd go". He still hesitated about undertaking what he called "a professional ministry".

However, having sought advice from home (which proved to be in favour of the Oxford post) and from Alfred Buxton (which was strongly critical of the proposal), at the end of what he described as 'a pretty good battering', he decided to accept the Principal's offer, still with the hope that after a minimum period of two years at the Hall some way might be found for him to serve the Ethiopian Church and its mission in its own country.

The nearest this hope came to an actual plan for the future was expressed in a letter written from Jerusalem when he went to stay with the Bishop and Mrs. Graham-Brown during the Easter vacation of 1933. He was greatly impressed by the Bishop's ministry and vision and he felt that he could happily work under his guidance. "The position is better than I could have hoped" he wrote, "for there is a regular attendance of about 70 monks (i.e. Abyssinians) here and pilgrims each year (up to 20). I had no idea whether there might not be only a dozen or so here altogether. When I mentioned what I had in mind to G.B., he said that actually he had been mentioning recently to his staff that the next thing to be done was to secure a liaison with the Abyssinians and so, although he couldn't offer me any money (the Diocese income has just been halved) the way is wonderfully open. The thing would probably be to go on with the language at Wycliffe Hall and try and prepare for or write some kind of B.D. thesis on the Abyssinian Church in some aspect. And then after 2 years (or 3) to return and get down to the job along the lines that opened." He could envisage all kinds of difficulties and obstacles which made it impossible to be explicit but it is clear that his heart had been captured by the Abyssinians and that he was ready to do everything possible to prepare himself to serve them in the future.

But the vision was never to be realised. First the wicked invasion of Abyssinia, then G. B's tragic death in a motor accident, finally the War, meant that Joe's eventual mission in Jerusalem was not to work amongst Abyssinians, nor under G. B's leadership, but as a Chaplain to the Forces with a special mission of another kind to fulfil.

4

Teacher and Evangelist

Joe joined the staff at Wycliffe Hall at a particularly auspicious period in its history.

In 1925 Graham-Brown was appointed Principal. At once he set to work to strengthen the Staff academically and soon secured as colleagues two men with first-class degrees — Julian Thornton-Duesbury in Greats and Theology, Verrier Elwin in English Literature and Theology. He was convinced that the Evangelical movement in the Church, while possessing a splendid tradition of evangelistic zeal and foreign missionary service, had failed to make any serious contribution to meeting the severe intellectual challenges to Christian faith of the past fifty years. Philosophers, historians and scientists had questioned accepted assumptions and Evangelicals seemed to have attempted little by way of reply. Graham-Brown sought to play a worthy part in the councils both of his Church and of the University and at the same time to keep the need for spiritual dedication in the forefront of the life of the Hall. His constant aim was also to instil into young men the sense of responsibility for doing their utmost to measure up to the high standards required for gaining recognition whether in academic circles or in the field of published work.

Yet with this new emphasis on responsible scholarship he did not neglect other important aspects of human experience. Probably his most memorable achievement during his Principalship, was first the conceiving of the idea of spending a vacation term in Palestine and then the carrying of it into actual realisation. Both in 1929 and in 1931 he led a large party of Wycliffe Hall students to Jerusalem where they lived for approximately six weeks, pursuing their studies and at the same time gaining intimate knowledge of the geographical and historical background of Biblical faith.

Joe was a member of the party that went out in 1929. This visit provided an uexpected and unwelcome adventure. Not only did the students learn about the sites of the Holy Land: they also witnessed at first-hand an outbreak of the bitter antagonism between Arab and Jew which has become all too familiar since 1929.

The Arab uprising took the authorities completely by surprise. On August 23rd. rioting broke out at about 1. p.m. and at tea in the afternoon Graham-Brown, who was quite fearless in face of emergencies, called upon the students to enrol as special constables, there being no adequate military presence in the city. At 4.30. p.m. Joe was amongst those who were enrolled (these included civil servants and retired business men), thus joining the company of those who in the words of a speech by the High Commissioner six weeks later "threw their private affairs to the winds, sometimes even leaving their own homes and families unprotected, and rushed to join the Special Constabulary to risk their lives for the protection of the lives and property of others".

He continued: "Had it not been for the support moral as well as physical which you gave to the handful of Police of the British Section who, at one moment were nearly all the force that stood between Palestine and anarchy, the country would have been on the brink of disaster; and, at best, the area of the disturbances would have been greatly extended and their duration indefinitely prolonged . . . How you left your homes and exposed yourselves to unknown risks and remained for days and nights at your posts without rest or relief will be recorded as a page of the history of Palestine and the memory of it will be remembered for all time".

This may sound like the rhetoric of a former colonial age but there can be no doubt that the Wycliffe Hall students encountered some quite terrifying experiences. Joe kept a brief diary of the days of their enrolment before reinforcements arrived and some extracts throw a vivid light on life in Palestine during the emergency.

August 24th. From midnight till after dawn we were on guard on the right of the Jaffa Road . . . expecting an Arab attack. We had one sniping shot — my first experience — which was much too near. We raided one house and captured one man with a revolver.

From about 8.30. a.m. to nearly 6. p.m. we were under fire till relieved by the armoured car at about 1.30. I got up on top of the synagogue roof early on and was incredibly glad to get down again by a rickety ladder as the shots were all too close; the trouble about our position was that there was no clear front and sniping from both sides. About noon there was a rush of Arabs and they got into the end of Mikor — Lavin and burnt two places. I thought we should have to clear out but the armoured cars settled things. About 2. p.m. we went up to an Arab house on the left which had been sniping, looking for 3 of our fellows who had gone up to Talpioth — we searched the place and were then fired on at about 15 yds range from behind — a near thing!

Ultimately we evacuated the Jews and were very glad to

leave ourselves about 5.30. p.m. (I was one of the last)''.

That evening and next day he was helping to convoy mails and milk, being fired on and returning fire: guarding Jews being evacuated on the Jaffa Road and bringing back wounded from Hebron.

"there was no trouble going but coming back the armoured car cleared two ambushes. I helped to carry the wounded to the cars and it was a dreadful business especially as they had to come back to Jerusalem in ordinary lorries. I saw the dead at the Hospital. There were I think 15 lorries full of about 50 wounded''.

During the week he was sometimes patrolling a threatened section (from midnight to 6.15. a.m.), sometimes acting as a street lamp-lighter, sometimes escorting those repairing telegraph wires — often in temperatures of over 100° F and often finding it hard to keep awake. Finally on August 31st., after going to Bethlehem and escorting eight sheiks back to prison ('I am glad they didn't cause any trouble') Joe and his fellow students were demobbed at about 11.30. p.m.

II

Graham-Brown was appointed Bishop in Jerusalem in 1932. His successor, J. R. S. Taylor brought a wide and varied experience to his new office as Principal and this was supplemented by the quite first-rate teaching ability of his Vice-Principal, Douglas Harrison. These were the two anchor men at Wycliffe over nearly ten years. Other members of staff served for shorter periods and amongst these was Joe who, during his three years, made a quite outstanding contribution. Different in temperament and methods from the Principal and Vice-Principal, he yet shared completely their fundamental aim to help men in every possible way to prepare themselves for their future ministry.

He returned home from Cairo in the summer of 1933, planning to be ordained in the autumn. But an operation for cholic and a period of recuperation in Switzerland delayed this until February 25th. when he was made deacon by the Bishop of Oxford at Cuddesdon. Regarding the ordination he wrote: "I am sure you must have prayed, because I really felt like laughing Sunday morning — it seemed such a funny position for me to be ordained — and yet quite inevitable and I had no trace of anxiety about its rightness . . . I had to read the Gospel in the service and got through fairly alright, except for one of my habitual pauses in the middle''. All this took place in the midst of a hectic first term in which Joe was exceedingly active in the University, leading 'squashes' in College or addressing student gatherings. At the Hall he had been allotted responsibility for teaching early Church History and the Old Testament: it soon became clear that the latter was to prove his major subject of interest.

This is not surprising seeing that his imagination had been captivated by his experiences in Egypt, Israel and Abyssinia. He had noted how many of the cultic traditions of the Ethiopian Church seemed to be reminiscent of the Old Testament while, in Egypt and Palestine, he had plenty of opportunities to learn about modern Jewry. What drew him most to the Old Testament, however, was its record of the life and work of the prophets, beginning with Moses. His own method of preaching, and even to a degree of lecturing, was to speak spontaneously out of a well-stored mind and through a colourful vocabulary, rather than by writing out a detailed script and using more traditional terms. He prepared himself continuously by eager reading and by expectant praying. Indeed he claimed that all the sermons preached during his time at Wycliffe were Spirit-inspired, composed while on his knees. Often he approached a particular occasion with no clear conviction about what he was to say. Yet he rarely failed to capture the imaginations and hearts of his hearers, even if logic and an ordered sequence were by no means obvious components.

This method of seeking direct divine inspiration and of listening to what God would say seemed to be precisely that of the Old Testament prophets. Joe had undergone the discipline of examining their books critically and historically but beyond that he wanted to convey to his hearers their sense of *God,* their discernment of His special actions in the world, their struggles with recurrent idolatries, their denunciations of injustice wherever found. He responded eagerly to commentators who, through the writings of the prophets, challenged the world of the 20th. century to hear the Word of God and to take appropriate action.

He made contact again with old friends who had been fellow-members of the O.I.C.C.U. and in August 1934 he contributed a letter to the bulletin of the Oxford Missionary Prayer Band. Other letters dealt fairly straightforwardly with work going on in parishes or on mission stations. But Joe, in characteristic fashion, looked back on his experiences of the past few months and tried to record the evidences of God's guiding hand in his personal affairs. The letter reveals much about the man.

"Most things in the last two years have gone contrary to

my expectations but out of — and despite — everything, there has crystallised the clear conviction that I am meant to do something for the Abyssinians. This conviction came to me over a year ago and as a result of it I felt able to accept the offer of work at Wycliffe.

"If I am to do what I want to do for the Abyssinians I must be ordained and so that problem was settled for me. I was to have been ordained on Sept 25. but actually I was put on the operating table the day before — which seemed good timing. Either chance or God; and being predestinationally inclined I believe it was God and if so I can take courage. If he is still sufficiently interested in me to intervene like that, then He will carry me through.

"In speaking of the future it is difficult not to fall into either 'presumptuous sin' or unbelief. And no experience of a call can do away with the necessity for faith. In fact I cannot but feel that it is only since that call that I have even begun to learn what faith is.

"My needs in the two year's interval before I can hope to do anything for the Abyssinians are great. I teach O.T. and tutorial work covers N.T. and Early Christian Doctrine and history as well. Preaching I find increasingly difficult. It is not from lack of opportunity but from failure to allow God to take the opportunities given, that we do not advance. Oxford is different altogether, both in religious, political and even I believe, philosophical outlook from four or five years ago.

"The change is for the better; it gives us a canvas. Can we on the canvas paint even the faintest resemblance of the figure of our Lord? 'His visage was so marred more than any man'. I saw, as never before, a year ago at Easter in Jerusalem when I lived a week with 'G.B.' that 'Greater love hath no man than this' is the daily principle of our Christian lives. Since I last wrote, I have failed Him often but, thank God He has said, Never will I fail you!''.

III

In the Michaelmas Term of 1934 a German missionary from the Basel mission was in residence at Wycliffe. Joe was enormously impressed by him. "Certainly those Germans who are standing up for the truth have a far clearer idea of the issues at stake than most of us over here have. He (Dr. Metzer) said that if anybody in Germany to-day lectured on the circumstances of the prophet's life, his date etc etc, nobody would go to attend his discourses. What they went for were those lectures which gave the prophet's message and applied it to the modern age. I am trying to do more of this. But with the Mission there is very little time to prepare''.

'The Mission', to which the letter refers, was the 1934 edition of an event which had become an annual feature at St. Aldate's Church, and was directed particularly towards freshmen. The fact that Joe was invited to be the Missioner showed that his special gifts as an evangelist had already been recognized. He gave a great deal of thought to his main topics while allowing himself a wide freedom in their delivery. Significantly he chose as over-all theme: *Personal Religion: An Adventure in Sincerity.* Each of the three words *personal, adventure* and *sincerity* denoted aspects of religious experience which to him were of crucial importance. What he was to learn later in a more comprehensive way from Martin Buber was already a firm conviction in his own mind: that the *I-Thou relationship,* whether between person and person or between man and God, is the ultimate determinant of every human existence. Again, though he never decried reason or the need for disciplined study, in the last resort Christian faith, he believed, had the nature of *adventure,* launching out into the unknown, taking a risk. Finally, the essential attitude, without which nothing worth while could ever be achieved, was that of *sincerity.* While still in Cairo he had written in one of his letters that in Evangelical circles there needed to be a thorough cleaning out of *hypocrisy.* So much was *said* which did not really correspond to the true state of affairs. Throughout his ministry he hated hypocrisy. He refused to cover up, even when his words might provoke feelings of resentment. He never tried to speak from a superior position, denouncing or blaming. He never spared *himself* in his efforts to achieve complete sincerity. He would have rejoiced in Lionel Trilling's classical analysis of Sincerity as the *sine qua non* of authentic human existence.

When it came to individual topics he chose such titles as: Dare I be sincere?: The Cross — God's sincerity: The Yes or No of sincere response. His addresses took the form of simple but vivid biblical expositions, focussed upon characters whose stories are told either historically or in parable: the Pharisee and the publican, the two thieves crucified with Christ etc. He appealed to his hearers for decisions between possibilities represented by pairs such as these and this resulted in some of his hearers committing themselves openly to Christian faith; it was clear that Joe's message and methods appealed to undergraduates and subsequently he was often in demand to lead similar efforts, either in universities or in parishes. He confessed to feeling quite exhausted, ''it cost me something and I hope it will have counted for God''. Probably it was this that his audiences came to recognize when he called upon them to make costly decisions. He poured himself out with complete sincerity, not counting the cost, only concerned to present the claims of Christ within a world which was becoming increasingly secular in its aims and values.

IV

Meanwhile, in the day-to-day work of teaching, he commended himself to students by his enthusiasms, his sparkling witticisms and his affectionate concern for individuals. One of them, Canon G. H. Donne Davis, wrote a letter in 1973, more than 35 years after leaving Wycliffe, in which he declared that although since his student days he had never met Joe again, "I have always ministered with the inspiration which he engendered. He had the great gift under the Holy Spirit of showing us our true selves but not leaving us there in bewilderment, but showing us clearly what we must do and the power in Christ which was available to us".

Having said that Joe's course of addresses on the Old Testament prophets was quite outstanding, making them come alive in a most vivid way, Canon Davis went on to quote from notes on a sermon preached in Chapel at that time which 'electrified' his hearers. This was its conclusion. "God's training is for now, not presently. His purpose is for this minute, not for something in the future. The Devil's delusion is that there is something better just round the corner. This causes us to give less than the best. It causes us to be dissatisfied — when I leave Wycliffe, when I am senior Curate etc. You cannot lead people further than you have got yourself. It involves discipline and holiness: 'for their sake I sanctify myself'.

"How can you prepare at Wycliffe for this task? How can Wycliffe be a means to an end? 1. By doing the thing I don't like. 2. By doing the thing I do like better. Are we funking the things we don't like. They, like St. Paul's thorn in the flesh, may be a more effective means of grace than any Sacrament.

"There is a danger in conforming to type — Mirfield Man, B.C.M.S. Man, Wycliffe Man, Neanderthal Man! Develop your own gifts. Dont't be mass produced and standardised. The Holy Spirit is yours. Christ is yours. Opportunities are yours. All things are yours and you are Chirst's. You must be adventurers in your vacations: scholars in term: saints always".

It was an exacting standard which he set before himself and before his students; and he was an exacting tutor so far as academic standards were concerned. Yet he never attempted to force spiritual issues or to impose his own interpretation of Christian discipleship on those struggling with doubts and difficulties. One who was tutored by Joe at Wycliffe has written:

> After two terms there, the whole Christian cause died on me and I decided to leave and take up some other career. The gentleness, the quiet understanding and concern of Joe, I have always remembered. No school-mastering or criticism and with great emptiness and confusion I went home for the Easter vacation and within a day or two I received a note from Joe that he and Padre Scott of St. Peter's Hall were taking a walking holiday in the Lake District — would I join them? I did, and, though to the best of my memory Joe never tried to open up on my problems during that week — darkness and despair evaporated and hope and belief were rekindled. So that I ever came into the ministry and have remained in it, goes back a lot to this occasion which I still gratefully remember.

And that which always endeared Joe to me — he always believed the best, hoped the best, was sure you would rise to the opportunity and not fail. That has had a power for me all my years. John Robinson, some little time ago, quoted some words from one of his father's books: ''large souls do not try to impose themselves upon us . . . in their presence we spread and feel strangely at home''. Those words surely can be said of Joe.

He might have stayed on at Wycliffe for he enjoyed his work and was at ease with other members of the Staff for whom he had a profound respect. The Hall was full to overflowing and can rarely have had a stronger or more varied team to guide its affairs. But he had initially come for a period of two years, hoping then to be able to re-consider the possibility of missionary service. Although, with the invasion of Abyssinia, this prospect receded and he remained at Wycliffe for a third year, by the end of that time he felt increasingly that he ought to move to some kind of parochial experience. At St. Aldate's Church in Oxford, the Rector, the Rev. F. S. Cragg, was feeling the strain of ministering both to a large town congregation as well as to undergraduates in term time and Joe seemed an ideal colleague to ease that strain, particularly in the responsible task of preaching. Though this was not perhaps the parish that he would have readily chosen, he gained a firm conviction that this was God's call and he accepted the Rector's invitation.

V

So there followed another three years of Joe's career, spent not so much in teaching basic information about the Bible — language and history and author's intentions — but in interpreting texts and in applying them to the circumstances of people living in the social and international tensions of the 1930's. Again it was the prophets who constantly stimulated him. He organised Tuesday afternoon groups for undergraduates and with them studied books of the Prophets. He assisted in preparing those going on student missions by relating biblical situations to their own anticipations. When the four hundredth anniversary of the setting up of the Bible in parish churches was being celebrated he enquired whether the University, with all its attention to academic courses on the Bible, was doing anything to further the prophetic and creative application of prophetic and evangelic truths to the critical problems of our own time.

This, he believed, was at least part of his own special vocation. He would try to apply Old Testament prophecy in a *personal* way or to the problems of international relations. As an example of the former he characterised Jeremiah as a man who had been deprived of all his props: his village, his family, the Temple, the City of Jerusalem, the Nation, the State "till in the end he was himself brought by innner and outer agony to their inward spiritual relation to God direct which he prophesies as the essence of the New Covenant in Chap 31. He antiquated the Old Covenant in that prophecy and was able to do so because it had already been antiquated in his own experience". He had in fact to *unlearn* something and, as Joe went on to comment, it is far easier in life to learn than it is to unlearn.

His foray into international affairs did not win so immediate a response "Yesterday I tried to do Hosea and had a peculiar time because 'Ephraim's a cake half-baked' I referred directly in application to British foreign policy to-day, with great and obvious wrath registered by one member of my audience: this reduced me to diminuendo and very soft pedal for the rest of the time, I didn't like it at all. However all is well, I think, now with the fellow, and though the reference was perhaps rash and impetuous, I think it was true. I wish I had more stomach for a fight. Then I should of course fight less! But I hate a real conflict and generally run away or fight on a wrong issue. I always so sympathise with Gairdner's remark (for a long time Temple Gairdner, the great missionary to the Muslim world had been one of Joe's heroes) in his biography about his need of physical courage. And if you haven't that, it affects everything else, mental, moral etc courage, I think. Yet 'courage' is not one of the fruits of the Spirit. So what are we to do?''.

At St. Aldate's Joe soon won the confidence of the regular city congregation. His sermons were always lively and the very fact that you never knew what he was going to say next stimulated attention. It was in personal relations, however, that he proved irresistible. He was so genuinely interested in people and entered so readily into their feelings in life's crises — births, marriages, deaths — that he was soon as well-known as a pastor as he was a preacher. He had an extraordinary knack of breaking down barriers of shyness and reserve in every kind of social environment. Without a trace of superiority, either of class or of learning, he drew people out and almost at once they felt completely at ease in his presence. Yet he was not aggressive. It was all spontaneous and natural: no pretense no hypocrisy.

VI

Throughout these fruitful years in Oxford, between his return from Egypt and his setting out on a new adventure, one problem of a personal kind was constantly troubling him. It did not often come to the surface but his letters to his mother reveal moments almost of exasperation as he tried to combine a complete loyalty and devotion with the establishment of his own independence of thought and feeling. He owed her so much, shared with her so much of the concern for the spread of biblical Christianity, felt so deep a responsibility for her as the only son of a widowed mother. He wrote to her with the utmost regularity and joined her during vacations either at Felixstowe or abroad.

But even when he had in a measure established his own freedom from a literalistic reading of the Scriptures and from the dogmatic fundamentalism which characterised his mother's home church at Felixstowe, there was still the question of possible marriage and of establishing his own freedom to relate to a type of femininity not necessarily the same as that represented by the Felixstowe circle. This was the possibility which suddenly arrested him when reading the passage in Luke 2 while in Abyssinia. Might it be necessary to 'break the custom', to relate to a different pattern than that in which he had for so long been nurtured?

Just before Christmas in 1935 he wrote very frankly about his differences from his mother's general outlook, while gladly admitting that they possessed much in common. She had evidently expressed concern from time to time about his veering towards 'Modernism', leading him in one letter to say sharply that he could see no justification for retreat to "an intellectually suicidal position. What is important is to recover the spiritual intimacy of touch with God, which is most difficult to keep and on which all else depends. I cannot feel that however often intellectual work may seem to knock a man off that, it must necessarily do so". Then at greater length, he summarized their differences by contrasting the natural and the supernatural.

"The difficulty is to live a really natural life on a truly supernatural plane. And I think there is danger either way of lopsidedness. As I looked down your family tree one can see the 'supernaturalness' toppled over into 'isms' and the naturalness becoming just un-Christian by reaction. I hope very much that we may as a family learn more to live together in a true Christian way. I cannot hope for any supernatural miracle in me to achieve this but I hope His grace may bring about that which nothing else can. This is not to say that I haven't been happy at home. But it is because I do feel that anti-modernist feeling you have and my differences with you — which I do not think are great — could be overcome in a real effort, or rather recognition, of Christianity as naturally supernatural. What you object to fundamentally is the denial of the supernatural. What I can't help objecting to in reply is the entirely unnaturalness of much of the so-called supernatural Christianity . . . You can help me beyond all words if you will move out to a common objective rather than from a dogmatic standpoint which may be right but becomes hard by repetition. Sometimes I regret to say I have almost wanted to run away from family life but Christmas reminds me that the family was the centre of Christ's life. And I hope this Christmas may mean that for us".

But there was a still deeper problem in his relationship with his mother and this came to the surface when in 1939 the suggestion was made to him that he should go as curate to Bishop Linton who had retired from Persia and was incumbent of a large Birmingham parish. A move to Birmingham was in some way associated with Mrs. Fison's need to leave Felixstowe. Might she herself move to Birmingham if Joe decided to undertake this new work? Would nearness in *space* help to overcome what she felt was some kind of barrier between herself and her son?

Joe answered categorically: "It's not space that matters: it's no good pretending that space saves the situation or loses it. If the feeling is there, it doesn't matter whether we are in different continents. I'm sure the issue is that true attachment i.e. love, must be free and therefore must be preceded by detachment, so that it can be freely made. And that detachment is not achieved by your staying in Felixstowe or my going to Handsworth (Birmingham) though that may be its temporary condition. It's an inward detachment. I have a feeling that this has been near the heart of our difficulties. And I think there is no doubt that it can be fully overcome if frankly faced. But I think it's no good my 'kidding' myself that I can be free by running away to Timbuctu or your imagining you leave me free by staying at Felixstowe. It is essentially a matter of the inward spirit. And the difficulty is to see this — which I feel I have only just begun to see — or it practically is. Either I ignore it or wail about it or SIN as a monster! in either case I do nothing about it. Naturally therefore the situation 'stays put'!!'". Then with a final reference to the vital issue being that of the *inward spirit* he left the matter without, he averred, the anxiety that he used to feel.

Honest as always, Joe expressed in this frank outburst a principle of profound theological as well as human importance. *True attachment must be free and therefore must be preceded by detachment.* It is at the very heart of the Christian gospel that God allowed man, whom he created and might have bound to himself, freedom to detach himself from the created relationship in order that he might, on his part, enter freely into a relationship of attachment and so experience true love. The breaking of any original attachment cannot help being painful. Yet Joe saw that only by such a painful detachment could a new and far more wonderful attachment be achieved, the experience of freely-given love. When he wrote his letter in the summer of 1939 he little dreamed that in roughly a year's time he would be leaving home and England and that this detachment would ultimately lead to a new attachment, interfused with pain, yet bringing an experience of a love such as he had never known before.

5

Freedom and the Future

In August 1940 the regular and relatively sheltered ministry which Joe had carried on with so great acceptance in Oxford came to an end. War had become a grim reality. Chaplains were needed. Joe was single and available. He enlisted and was told to report to a Chaplains' training establishment near Chester. Here 35 men from different denominations met together for a fortnight and Joe responded immediately to the spiritual vitality of the place. "Don't worry about me" he wrote to his mother: "who now has much less to worry him than before he put on khaki, for all things are ordered for me". Over many months he had been uncertain about his next move. Now for a period of five years the place and programme of his work would be decided for him.

From Chester he proceeded to his first appointment at the Oudenaarde Barracks in Aldershot. His duties were mainly to visit men in hospital and in detention, a task which he found very interesting and offering good opportunities "though I simply can't make a stereotyped Evangelical opening gambit". He had time for reading the early Fathers and for occasional visits to Oxford. His mother was evidently anxious about moral standards in army life — cards and drink in particular. He assured her in a letter that he was neither a card-sharper nor a wine-bibber but simply asked for her trust in these matters. "I thought a lot about the question of teetotalism and I really feel that to be a rigid teetotaller would be (for me) the easy way out. Anyhow the question came up in a concrete issue — an officer asked me to have a glass of port one evening which I did. And I felt God ratified it almost immediately when same officer opened up his heart almost at once in a way I very rarely have experienced".

During the uncertainty of waiting for what might be a more permanent assignment an event occurred which moved him very deeply. His friend Alfred Buxton, while in London with his brother, was in the Church House when it was struck by a bomb and they were both killed instantly. Mrs. Buxton telephoned Joe and this enabled him to be present at the funeral at Brookwood, not far away. He had an enormous admiration for Alfred, even though they were very different in temperament and in some aspects of their theological outlook. In a memorable tribute to him, which incidentally revealed something about himself, Joe wrote:

"To me Alfred was always coming and going. I remember him coming into the hotel to meet me in Djibouti in July 1932. Still more vivid is the photo in my album of his leaving me behind at Dirre Dawa two months later. And from then till his arrival at Didcot Station last July in pouring rain (by the wrong train!) and the final going off from Oxford in August — all the way through, like his Master, he never used an arrival platform except for a new departure.

"The Master left Heaven for earth — did the angels criticize? He left Capernaum for 'other cities also' — did the local church object? He set His face to go from Galilee to Jerusalem — the disciples were against it and what did Mary think? He left the right hand of the thief for the right hand of the Father — and now who can dispute the claim of Him who 'came not to be ministered unto but to minister and to give His life a ransom for many'?.

"Alfred would never have claimed the infallibility of his Master. Many, he knew, were his own errors. Impetuous, visionary? Yes. But over and above all else here was a man 'not disobedient to the heavenly vision' who in himself was greater than all he did. For him the joy of 'Well done!': for his family and friends the loss of a leader and a great pioneer: for all the call of the One Lord to rise up and follow in 'the power of an endless life'".

II

After weeks of rumours and uncertainties the exciting news came on Jan 12th. 1941 that he was to be posted overseas, possibly to Cairo. Probably there was nothing he could have desired more. He would be back amongst friends in a familiar place: he would be closely related to the North African campaign: he might even get to the frontier of Abyssinia. It would be a long journey around the Cape and he did not actually arrive in Egypt until the later part of April. But the voyage out was full of interest and there were no alarms from enemy action.

Leaving England in the middle of February, the first port of call was Freetown where they sweltered in the steamy heat of Sierra Leone. By a happy coincidence, a St. Aldate's curate had come out to a College in the city two years previously and with him as guide Joe was able to make the most of his time on shore. Back on board he offered a course of six lectures on *Christianity and Western Civilisations* — a new departure for him which he worked out in a Toynbee-like way, claiming to discern a recurring pattern which he described as Freedom, Law and Breakdown. Freedom was the key-word. For the prophets of Israel, Freedom of the Spirit. For the philosophers of Greece, Freedom of the Mind. But in each case freedom was succeeded by law and formalism and ultimately by some kind of breakdown.

Through Jesus Christ an altogether new freedom was made available to mankind but again Christian history, Joe claimed, has witnessed the same recurring pattern of new discoveries of freedom succeeded by law and logic and then breakdown. The lectures drew increasing numbers and were immensely stimulating for his own thinking. Lacking the possibility of constantly referring to books he felt that he was being compelled to think for himself in a new way. Later in the voyage he turned to the Gospels, lecturing on the life and teaching of Jesus, first as recorded by Mark and then by Matthew.

His cabin companions turned out to be a Church of Scotland padre, a Roman Catholic priest and a Free Church minister. They got on famously together and all in all it seems to have been a happy ship. There was a welcome call at Durban with Joe enjoying visits to St. Paul's Church and some of its congregation (here the war seemed very far away), the surroundings reminding him of Maadi in Egypt where his mother had stayed while he was at Cairo College: 'soft air, quietness, grasshoppers and frogs'. Also "the Zulus have been a great attraction and I have been twice to their Reserve. A fine race they seemed, when uncontaminated with civilisation. But how to get the child peoples to rise to adult life and nationhood is a tremendous problem". Surf bathing and a united Parade Service on the Test Match Cricket Ground, with Joe using a microphone for the first time ever, were amongst the memorable experiences of this interlude on shore.

But at length the long voyage ended, in many ways to Joe's regret. "The great thing has for me been the really wonderful opening among the men. I followed up my blackboard talks on Christianity and Western Civilisation with four lectures on the life of Jesus according to St. Mark. Then latterly we've discussed some subject nearly every day and then again after supper at 8 p.m. The men seemed to drink it in and they weren't a religious clique at all. There really has been a wonderful response and I hope it may be a line I can continue when I get wherever I do on shore. The preparation of the talks has been very good for me and prevented my ever being a bit bored with a voyage which I reckon would have cost me £450 in peace time!". More than two years were now to be spent in the familiar surroundings of a city to which he already felt deeply attached.

III

He arrived in Cairo at a time when some 65,000 troops were in the area, cared for by a dozen Chaplains. During his early months, his main responsibility was that of chief chaplain to a very large hospital unit though he also conducted camp services. The hospital was housed in a palatial hotel and this did not make visiting easy as there were few large wards. However it was work that he greatly enjoyed, especially as he was constantly discovering links with home parishes. In the city at large there were numerous friends, either engaged in some kind of war service or connected with the College in which he had taught ten years previously. He was soon called on to give lectures in the Cathedral on the Old Testament and all in all the general situation in which he found himself could hardly have been more congenial.

Yet there were certain unresolved personal tensions in his life which were not of the creative kind out of which new visions and energies are born. He was anxious about marriage and his relationship with women: anxious too about the ambivalent relationship with his mother. He wanted counsel not primarily of a spiritual but of a psychological kind and to whom better could he turn than to his friend since Abyssinian days, Dr. Marcus Gregory, who was then practising in Cairo?

A number of visits were arranged in which he spoke frankly of his problems without being subjected to a lengthy analysis. As a result he experienced a new sense of personal freedom, the quality about which as an ideal and as an experience in the lives of individuals and of societies he had so frequently spoken. And this new sense manifested itself in a quite remarkable way, a way to which I personally know no parallel. During the month of October 1941 he literally poured out a succession of rhyming poems and then stopped, never again producing anything of the same kind. These poems were collected together and printed in Cairo to form a booklet entitled *Freedom and the Future*. He read some of them to friends: some he wrote out in full in minute handwriting and sent back to England. The vocabulary is not remarkable: the themes are not original: the altogether impressive feature is the rhythm, which seems like a dance in words to celebrate the new prospect ahead.

In the letter accompanying one of the poems sent to his mother he wrote: "Here is an effusion if you can read it. I am quite astonished at it and rather thrilled though it must be full of poetic howlers. (On one of the copies he wrote: Dreadful Doggerel) I've had two days straight fever and this morning this came straight out and the fever has, I think, left me! It's certainly what at this moment I feel''. This first poem he entitled *The March of Freedom* and it ran to no less than 210 lines of rhyming pairs. Ostensibly it celebrated the resistance of the Russian 'peasants' in face of Hitler's onslaught:

They died upon the plainlands 'twixt the White Sea and the Black
They gave their lives this summer and they didn't turn their back
They were simple Russian peasants and they only knew one thing,
Their country was in danger and they served another king
Than Hitler, the Dictator, who led the Teuton hordes
And promised Europe freedom.

But the simple Russian peasant didn't quite agree with this,
He knew that fighting's futile and it doesn't bring you bliss;
He'd had his lesson taught him in the '14-'18 war
And he didn't need another to teach him any more;
But there's something worse than dying and there's something worse than war
And that's the lack of freedom.

So the stanzas continue, often repetitive, recalling past freedom-fighters such as Drake, Cromwell and even the leaders of the French Revolution of 1789, heroes such as Gordon and Mallory and Captain Scott, returning again and again to the peasants on the Russian plains and concluding:

Now if the Russian future could be blended in with ours,
And if the Russian spirit could give us back the powers
That come from looking forward, however crude maybe
The future that we look for, the outlines that we see,
Then God indeed will triumph and men indeed will say
He still performs His wonders in His own mysterious way.

Other poems strike a more explicitly religious and Christian note, celebrating the loving purpose of God whose service is perfect freedom and His entrance into the human situation so that by his sharing our lot we might share His victory. One remarkable re-telling of the story of the man who had lain for 38 years by the pool of Bethesda and then responded to the words "Rise, take up thy bed and walk" occupies nearly forty four-lined stanzas: Joe was then in his thirty-sixth year and one wonders whether he was identifying himself with the man who leapt into a new freedom

For Jesus disclosed to all whom he healed
By the might of his conquering will
That the heart of a man, if it's only unsealed
Can go forward to victory still.

Perhaps the most unexpected celebration of all is the one in praise of music. There was certainly a love of music and musical accomplishment in the family but Joe was not a performer himself nor had he been a concert-goer. Yet in the poem entitled *Music* (which he copied out before printing and sent to his Aunt Connie) he assigns to this form of art the highest place.

We need a new arousing of the spirit of our race
And it's surely the musicians who will set the fastest pace
By the lessons that they teach us of the harmony of God
Achieving transformations of the crudest earthbound clod,
To be reached through strife and warfare and the agony of soul
That's the lot of every artist who attempts to reach his goal.

The final poem on *The Future,* written on October 26, concludes with these lines:

So dream on of the future, but face up to the task
And don't let dreams of pleasure life's sterner duties mask:
Let's build our garden cities and abolish every slum,
But don't let constant toiling turn cheerful faces glum,
For the struggle for the future is the struggle of our God
And He sacrificed His leisure and He didn't think it odd
That only by long striving and the willingness to die
Could God be proved triumphant and the Devil's dope a lie.

More than once Joe uses the adjective 'crude'. Many of his rhymes and comparisons could be called crude. Many of his themes could be called imperialistic propaganda. Many of his references to Russia could, in the light of hindsight, be called naive or starry-eyed. Yet the phenomenon remains — for less than a month a stream of rhyming couplets flows with the utmost freedom and then dries up. What he had learned from the study of history and from the experiences of living in the Thirties provided him with much of his material but the shaping was his own achievement. Did he project on to world-events his own release into a new freedom and a new vision of the future? No one can tell; but that some critical change took place about this time in Cairo seems certain. And one piece of evidence is that shortly thereafter he made a proposal of marriage. It was rejected. For the moment he had failed to win the prize. 'Cast down' he wrote 'but not in despair'. At least he had discovered the way to enjoy natural relationships with women. He had to wait another two years before freedom and the future gained its symbolic realisation in a joyful engagement.

IV

In February 1942 he was posted to another job in the area. It was for him, he wrote, a radical change. "I'm very busy as musician, iconoclast, church goer, landscape gardener, painter, decorator, gramophone player, foreman of works, payer of workmen, contractor, designer, and I don't know what else! All this is very good for me as it keeps the old mind looking forward and not back and that's half or more than half the essence of life, I think . . . I have to go to church very often and get up early. Horrid! I've very little use for Lent! However the outstanding thing is that the war is giving me switch over after switch over of thought, work, interest etc so that the old horizons and outlooks seem sometimes very far away. I wonder where it all is leading but I can't doubt that it is leading somewhere, however chaotic and disordered the course may be through my indiscipline and perverseness".

He was evidently entrusted with the task of adding an Institute to an existing church building — a place for recreation and for more informal religious activities. He revelled in the new job. "It's extraordinary how very much alive I am. I'm playing tennis better than for many years and am thoroughly enjoying the landscape gardening etc. And we had over 40 to the second discussion after Church yesterday evening. Shall we have a dance? or a whist drive? or a prayer meeting? or a lecture? or a billiard tournament? — you can imagine how out of my depth I am. Still it's great fun and a great opportunity. I'm feeling very rebellious against lots of past traditions, customs and inhibitions and I should like to feel that I had the courage to do (as well as write about) many foolish things. But I really am a very timid and cowardly soul. However I am not going back into the old rut, if I can help it! I still think Browning and Beethoven and Russia are a good combination".

Joe was not the only one who, in the midst of war conditions, determined not to go back into the old rut and yet who, when war was over, found it far from easy to find alternatives to the "traditions, customs and inhibitions" of the past. In Cairo he was free to experiment, to strike out on new lines and particularly to be in touch with every aspect of 'secular' life. "I go my independent way" he wrote, "buying a radiogram and records to play on it (including Beethoven's Emperor Concerto) searching all the city for carpets and finally finding the factory and giving a rotten talk on Thursday on Modern Affairs: thoroughly enjoying an extempore unprepared talk on Friday on Encouraging Signs of God's working to-day — the final point being (after 14 positive illustrations) that far away the most important is not any of these conversions to the Church and Christ but rather the evidence of the Church being converted to the world! I felt I had the wind behind me". Would he find the Church converted to the world back in England?

This was an exciting period. Then came an unwelcome and unsettling break. The 'tummy' began to misbehave itself and Joe found himself in hospital, at first rather enjoying the rest and attention but then being subjected to an excruciatingly painful examination. He had had trouble previously in Egypt and it was suspected that constant heat prevented the kidneys from operating properly. He was faced therefore with the prospect of possible surgery and in any case of being moved to a cooler climate. "I'm more or less resigned to it now" one letter said: "though I was quite dumbfounded and speechless when it was first mentioned — very full of wrath". Visitors flocked in to see him, he played a lot of chess and waited for the verdict, not without anxiety.

Then to his unbounded delight a reprieve came. The doctors decided that there were no stones after all. The 'appalling' and 'unmentionable' investigation had revealed that although little crystals had been forming inside him, this condition could be remedied simply by drinking a lot more. "You can imagine me now drinking like a fish unmentionable brands of the fieriest oriental liquors!". So he could leave hospital and after a few days' sick leave return to his work. The experience of being a patient caused him to reflect in a new way on the job of a hospital padre. What really impresses you in sick visitors? "I think the three things that matter most are (1) their coming at all (2) their interest in you (3) their inner spirit — certainly not what they say — and fortunately I've not had any preaching visitors!". How true this was of his own relationships with others. He could say the most outrageous things and yet the 'inner spirit' prevailed over anything he may have said.

In August there came another move, this time to the Royal Artillery base and he found himself in the sand under canvas, near his old job geographically but responsible for quite a different kind of work: "swamped with personal interviews of all sorts, I pontificate merrily on subjects of which I know nothing". He was full of admiration for men who really got things *done* e.g. the local director of all the Camp cinemas whose office was humming with life and vitality. "I think LIFE is the first thing: LOVE is the second. O.T. is LIFE. N.T. is LOVE. But N.T. presupposes O.T. and must have it for its background. That's why I feel very impatient of the church in all its deadness".

The celebration of *life* occurs again in a letter of January 1943. "I'm impressed by my own total ignorance about everything upon which I used to be (probably still am) most dogmatic. It's so fascinating meeting people of all sorts who, whatever else they are or are not, are at least alive. I am sure that is the first thing in the Bible, everyone is alive (except a few Kings) and then the distinction came between good and bad. The lifelessness and woodenness and lack of vitality of so much church — going and — goers I hate!! Let's lose our life (on all fronts and in every way) then we'll find it . . . I'm finding the Base Depot of the Gunners a good chance of meeting officers as well as men and so making up for some of the gaps which I think a perverted idea of religion let me in for in Varsity days. Anyhow it sometimes seems delightfully like starting life all over again. I've very little room for a great many things that once seemed important and you were on the right track when you told me to hurry up and find the right person. But that is much easier said than done. And so there is chaos on all fronts".

Anyone reading his letters written during this period cannot but feel a new sense of 'life and vitality' and confidence. They abound in the off-the-cuff reflections and remarks which all who knew him (except the most conservative and conventional) loved to hear. "I feel very doubtful about vast theologies (especially feminine!)". "Bombard the reactionaries — ecclesiastics especially". "I champ and storm at the incredible dullness or lack of initiative of many". "I have given up Calvin who talks on and on as if he knew everything about everything". "The worse the rebel at Wycliffe the better the padre now! Or so it appears". "I had a glorious time attacking all and sundry last week at a meeting mostly for padres on the subject 'Worship and Society to-day' ". (One of his assistant Chaplains, formerly a country parson, found all this pretty bewildering: with another, 'a fizzing High Church young parson', ex-agnostic and excellent chess-player, Joe got on famously even though 'I couldn't take the Holy Communion in the way he does in a month of Sundays') "The great thing about the Bible is — it hardly ever looks back to Eden and the blessed time (in fact it hardly ever mentions it): it is always looking forward".

The theme of looking forward continues in his letters. "I feel no desire to go back. (The suggestion was made that he might return to Oxford as Rector of St. Aldate's when it fell vacant in 1943) How stupid to have put myself in such a ridiculous prison house of phantasy and isolation — I get so angry as I look back! — and I feel as I look forward that I really know absolutely nothing. Of course I'm still bad — noisy and dogmatic. But inwardly how different I feel from E.M.C. and Wycliffe . . . I think to go with a unit would be very good for me — to know more officers personally. How futile life is without friendship! And how absurd a religion of compensation!".

As it turned out Joe was never to go out into the desert with a unit. He was kept busily employed with great parade services (1,000 men), with Religious Brains Trusts, organising concerts and musical recitals, taking Camp Prayers in the open air at 6.45 a.m. (he had prayers printed with the opening words 'The Lord thy God walketh in the midst of thy Camp: therefore shall the Camp be holy') writing notes for the troops on the life and teaching of Jesus, planning a great united service for Easter Day with East Africans, Egyptians, American blacks singing spirituals, Swiss and Greeks taking part — as he wrote, he was certainly unlikely to have a fuller job than that in the base camp. But he was not destined to remain there much longer. First there was to be a thrilling three weeks' leave in Palestine and soon after a decision by authority which was to provide still another creative forward move in his career: he was to take up residence in Jerusalem as Senior Chaplain to the Forces in that area. The consequences would be far-reaching.

6

'Journeys end in lovers meeting'

The posting to Jerusalem in the late summer of 1943 led directly or indirectly to momentous consequences for Joe. It brought him the immeasurable enrichments of

(a) An intimate knowledge of the 'Holy Land'.

(b) Intimate relationships with the 'Holy People'.

(c) A wife and first-born child.

It also saw the appearance in print for the first time of his own interpretation of New Testament faith.

I

So far as army protocol was concerned the move signified promotion. He now became Senior Chaplain in Jerusalem and, towards the end of his time, responsible for a still wider area. As far as administration was concerned, it is widely admitted that this was not his strong point and his office would probably have been in a sad disarray had it not been for the faithful assistance of a secretary. This man, a Jewish refugee from Europe, was a brilliant violinist but could not make his living as such. He therefore took the job of secretary and, having rescued from the waste-paper basket many documents which Joe had assigned to oblivion, set to work to create proper files and to restore order. The relationship was not unlike that between Bertie Wooster and the long-suffering Jeeves. On a famous occasion a caller arrived at the moment when Joe burst out from his office crying: "Mr. Bernstein, I am about to commit suicide!". "What, again Sir?".

The authorities had been wise enough to see that Joe's special training and teaching in the literature of the Old Testament could be turned to advantage for the refreshment and renewal of tired chaplains. Plans were worked out for bringing to Jerusalem chaplains of all denominations (except Roman Catholic) for refresher courses. They came from the North African desert and from as far afield as Italy: Joe was commissioned to organise the programme for their visit to the Holy Land based on St. George's Hostel, Jerusalem.

He accepted this new assignment with enthusiasm. He loved to travel and to visit ancient sites: he loved equally to learn about their history. A typical programme therefore lasted ten days: five or six days residence in Jerusalem with lectures by scholars from the neighbourhood, the remainder of the time with visits to places of interest (biblically and historically) throughout the Holy Land. He refused to get into a rut by following the same routine each time. Instead, he was always seeking to devise some new itinerary and to make sure that on every visit he would himself see something new. He was so successful in this that he was asked to devise a pattern for regular Palestinian guides and to draw up tests which might be used to give them accreditation.

The chaplains who came in to the courses were quickly welded into a company of friends by Joe's own friendliness and by his methods of mixing them up together in an informal way. They admired his obvious knowledge of the Scriptures, particularly the Old Testament, and his ecumenical spirit which not only surmounted denominational allegiances but which introduced members of the courses to Jews, Abyssinians, Copts, Russians and Greeks with their varying types of worship. Some years later when back in England he wrote:

"What a liturgical feast Jerusalem offers. Abyssinians worshipping with umbrellas and praying crutches, Greek orthodox extempore preaching on the site of Calvary and in the church of the Holy Sepulchre, the Latin Patriarch riding into Jerusalem on a donkey on Palm Sunday, the ceremony of the foot washing in Holy Week and the Armenian service of the Second Advent — and I have not said a word about Syrians, Copts, Protestants or even Anglicans!".

Joe made sure to introduce members of the Courses to whatever was 'going on' during their period of residence. He had a genius for making friends with those of other races, even if he did not know their language and this smoothed the way for his visiting chaplains to share experiences which would not otherwise have come their way. They responded to his enthusiasms and enjoyed to the full the spirit of camaraderie which he managed to create.

Something of his own 'feeling' for the Holy Land can be gauged by some paragraphs which he wrote in 1955 for an English group about to go on pilgrimage.

"Everything you see in Palestine is full of history, from Jericho (the most ancient city in the world, some say) to the Horns of Hattin, where the Crusaders fought their last desperate fight, down to Nebi Samwil, where the British fought in the first world war, and so to the new golden aluminium roof of the Dome of the Rock in Jerusalem (Jordan) and the second new Hebrew University in Jerusalem (Israel).

"Palestine is full of archaeology. Everyone now knows of Qumran (and the Scrolls). But there is also the Jebusite wall of Jerusalem, the hill of ancient Samaria, the thrilling site of Shiloh, and the tunnel — mind you go through it! — dug between the spring of Gihon and the pool of Siloam in the reign of Hezekiah. Then there is the oak of Mamre (how old is it?) and the cave (but you cannot go in!) of Machpelah at Hebron. There is Michmash — you can still see where Jonathan and his armour bearer climbed up, if you have got the energy to walk there! History awaits the archaeologist everywhere and if the archaeologist is any one at all like the great Dominican, Père de Vaux, then every stone of the Holy Land becomes a thrill.

"The little things all come alive: and so do the big things. You can see the stones of the Temple Wall. You can sit on Jacob's well: you can go into the synagogue (when was it actually built?) of Capernaum. You can go into the cave at Bethlehem — where Jesus may have been born. You can look out over the plain of Esdraelon from Nazareth — where Jesus was brought up. Jordan is there, filthy and foul — just as it was when Jesus was baptized in it. Galilee is there, beautiful and gay and green in spring — that is where Jesus taught. Jerusalem is there and so must also be the Green Hill, where Jesus died and rose again. But it does not look green, and where is it, actually? In the Church of the Holy Sepulchre or at 'Gordon's Calvary' or where? Go and look at the great stones at the bottom of the Freres school in the extreme N.W. corner of the Old City, before you make up your mind. 'The Bible comes alive' in the Holy Land: it does, indeed.''

Knowledge gained in this way was also to serve him in good stead when after returning to England he was asked to write a book on *Understanding the Old Testament* to be used specially in schools for teachers and senior pupils. His first chapter gives an admirable picture of the main geographical features of Palestine and creates a sense of the fascination of the country itself. He could move easily in the Old Testament writings just because he could imagine the contexts and the situations where the events took place. Probably no one in post-war England knew the details of the topography and historical geography of Palestine better than Joe.

II

On the very day on which I am writing about Joe and the 'Holy People' the radio brings an extended report of the bomb outrage in Paris outside a Jewish synagogue. There is great indignation that groups of anti-Semites should find it possible to operate so freely and to plant a bomb which might have killed scores on their way out from the sabbath-evening service if it had exploded minutes later. But it is not only neo-fascists who have been guilty of anti-semitism and the long record lies heavily on the consciences of Christian people. The tension between Jew and Christian has been one of the saddest features of the life of the past 2,000 years.

This tension, however, seemed to place no serious obstacle in Joe's path. He was determined to make friends with Jews wherever possible, to seek their help in interpreting the Holy Land and the Old Testament, and to invite a group of Jews to meet for friendly conversation and discussion with his fellow-chaplains. The response was remarkable. ''We were received as friends'' one of the rabbis said. And on this memorable occasion Joe was able before they separated, to bid all to prayer. This is how he describes the occasion and how it came about:

''During the war a group of Jews was talking over tea in new Jerusalem about the problem of making friends with the British troops then in Palestine. On being asked my opinion as to how this could best be done I replied, 'Stop making friends with them for an ulterior motive' (i.e. to make them pro-Zionist). I went on to point out that it was this ulterior motive that was the very thing they (rightly) hated in some forms of Christian missionary effort.''

As a sequel to this, a number of Jews were invited to meet a number of British chaplains and others at St. George's Cathedral Close, Jerusalem. A long tea party lasted from 4.30 to 6.30 p.m. and was ended in a silence that could be felt with the prayer that 'the peace of God' might be with 'the people of God'.'' Joe had no doubt that the Jews were, by divine providence, a holy people (The title of Chapter 5 in *Understanding the Old Testament* is *The Holy People: The Jews*). Yet this very recognition constituted one of the major tensions of his life: how to give glad assent to their peculiar calling and at the same time to be faithful to the tradition of St. Paul and St. Stephen in claiming that they had rejected the Messiah whom God had sent.

What remained most vividly in his memory from the St. George's meeting was the presence and words of the Hebrew philosopher and theologian, Biblical scholar and mystic, Martin Buber. ''The outstanding memory of that tea party is the moment when Professor Buber got up, a little man with a patriarchal beard, and told how he had heard a poor Jew in Eastern Europe praying in Yiddish that sounded like 'Gottener' the word that we know as 'Abba' or even 'Daddy'. 'That' said Professor Buber 'is real religion'''.

Whether this was his first contact with Martin Buber I do not know. One thing however is clear. No man in all his experience made a profounder impression on him. He would refer to him as 'the greatest man I have known'. Buber's books became his companions. His interpretation of the call of Moses became definitive for Joe's own interpretation of Old Testament theology. The famous phrase, used as a book-title by Dr. J. H. Oldham, 'Real life is meeting' expressed as succinctly as any words could Joe's own deepest conviction.

In an essay on Buber he expressed something of his own indebtedness.

''He does not attempt to take us out of the ordinary world but he does attempt to give to this ordinary world a new dimension of meaning. It is not things as things that really matter any more than it is ideas as ideas. It is things in relation to other things, and still more persons in relation to other persons. It is only in relationship that, in the deepest sense of the word, we are''.

Again in another essay he tried to apply Buber's insights to the English situation to which he (Joe) had returned. ''Ordinarily we live enclosed in shells of protective mechanism preventing our exposure to the disturbing personal contacts of real meeting. It is easy to illustrate this attitude. A member of a political party just represents his party point of view. An Evangelical just talks his traditional theology . . . A parent just discusses his little child. This is no real personal conversation at all. But it is quite different when two people suddenly drop their masks and speak heart to heart. It is quite different when a poet looks at a beautiful flower or scene, the significance of which overwhelms him. It is quite different when God meets us in the burning bush, in the Temple, or by the lakeside. In such meeting with the 'Thou' the depths of the 'I' are broken up and the fullness of meaning glimpsed. And by such things, Buber says, men live, in the real sense of that word, live''.

These essays not only throw light on Buber: they show what had become the very heart of Joe's own theology and message and outlook. He is already adumbrating what Ian Ramsey was to speak of as 'cosmic disclosure'. He is already advocating the use of true dialogue (he uses the word) in the practice of Christian missionaries. He never tried to write an extended theology from the perspective of persons in relation but this was the recurring theme in his Biblical expositions and his evangelistic addresses. And in his pastoral work he never tried to dominate the other or to force an issue: to meet, to share, to open doors, to expose himself to whatever might come in the encounter, was to carry out in practice what he had learned from Martin Buber.

Buber has been called prophet and mystic and Joe might have been given the same designations. Buber had no use for any mere abstractions or conceptual facades. As prophet, he spoke the word of God in a particular historical situation. As mystic, he experienced the divine presence in the encounters and activities of everyday life. In a remarkable tribute to Martin Buber, referring to the dialogues which he had been privileged to share with him, Paul Tillich once wrote: ''In these dialogues, as in almost all encounters with Martin Buber, something happened which transcended for me in importance the dialogue itself. It was the experience of a man whose whole being is impregnated by the experience of the divine presence. He was, as one might say, 'God-possessed'. God could never become an 'object' in Martin Buber's presence. The certainty of God always preceded the certainty of himself and his world. God, for him, was not an object of doubt, but the presupposition, even of doubt. This is the only way, I believe, which makes a dialogue possible with those who doubt and even with those who deny God. But this presupposes a universalism like that of Martin Buber''.

It was this kind of quality, I think, which laid hold of Joe. It was the quality of one of the great Old Testament prophets. He wanted a comparable conception of the living God to undergird or precede all his own efforts to bear witness to Him Who fulfilled God's preparation and God's promises. He could no longer begin with dogmatic affirmations of Christian faith which seemed to be the legacy of Greek and Roman

Christendom. He wanted rather to recapture the Hebrew celebration of God acting in the here and now of historic event and personal experience, acting to bring all such events and experience to their true significance and fulfilment through the Christ of the Cross and the Resurrection.

I think Joe would have seen his own task as being in some way comparable to that which Buber once expressed in very simple terms as being his own:

"I have no teaching. I only point to something. I point to reality. I point to something in reality that had not or had too little been seen. I take him who listens to me by the hand and lead him to the window. I open the window and point to what is outside. I have no teaching but I carry on a conversation".

III

Through war-service in Jerusalem Joe gained an intimate knowledge of the high-ways and by-ways of the Holy Land. He also gained invaluable insight into the nature of the Hebrew mind and the traditions of the Holy People through his friendship with Martin Buber. But by far the most significant outcome of his residence in the Holy City was the personal fulfilment which came to him through his falling in love with Monica Irene Stober, their engagement and marriage, and the birth of Carolyn, their first child.

Irene, whom Joe had first met when on sick-leave in Jerusalem from Egypt, was a kindergarten teacher. At that time, however she was teaching half-time at the British Community School, was one of the two Jerusalem censors of incoming and out-going telegrams, helped the Czech Consul with the public speeches he had to give in English, coached his little son, and taught English to classes of Czech refugee adults and children. She also wrote and took part in children's programmes of the Palestine Broadcasting Society. Joe was attracted by her vitality. Loving children himself, he was impressed by her understanding of children and their trust of and love for her. As they came to know one another he found many other links and things they had in common. Her father, Matthew Z. Stober, the founder of the Angola Evangelical Mission, was one of those evangelical missionary pioneers whom Joe had so greatly admired, willing to give up all worldly security and to face danger in order to carry the gospel to those they were called to serve. Her mother, before Irene was born, had also been on the mission field. (It was a 'faith-mission', which meant missionaries had no guaranteed salary but trusted

God to meet their needs). So the religious atmosphere of her home had been evangelical, missionary minded and Keswick Convention oriented, and, although her father was still alive, he had been so seldom at home that she, too, had been brought up by her mother alone. However, the influence of her grand-parents, aunts, and other relatives on her mother's side had brought in another element. They were Quakers, so the children were also taken to Meeting, and their grandfather paid for Irene and her sister's education at a Quaker boarding school. (There was the odd coincidence that both Joe and Irene were called by one of their names at home and the other by their friends elsewhere.) Finally, they each suffered the inner distress of loving and admiring their parents, while being unable to accept the narrowness of their theology. Each had, in different ways, stepped out of line in the eyes of their parents, but had never lost their faith in God or their desire to serve Him.

They were engaged just before Christmas 1943 and the marriage was arranged to take place in August 1944. Unhappily, however, the news of the engagement caused consternation in England. Both in fiction and in actual experience the general situation is common enough, where a mother, particularly a widowed mother, either rejects the thought of her son being married or believes she has a clear idea of the type of woman who would be suitable for him. Mrs. Fison was eager that her son should marry, but (like most Evangelicals) hoped that his choice would fall on someone sharing her own tradition and general outlook.

War conditions made it impossible for her to meet Irene, but it was clear that the latter was not bound by standards of relationship to the 'world' which were normative within conservative evangelical circles. Joe himself had felt delighted that his fiancée was "a modern girl" with an open mind, a sincere faith and a daring spirit, but his mother's frequent, anxious letters, begging him to break off the engagement, shook his certainty — not as to whether he loved Irene, but as to whether he could marry her against his mother's wishes. Could the freedom he had won in Egypt stand up to this final practical test?

So, with all the immense satisfaction derived from the Chaplains' courses and with all the joyful experiences associated with the meeting of lovers, (from this time on Shakespeare's *Journeys end in lovers meeting* became one of his most often quoted lines) there came also for them both a period of deep pain and, for Joe in particular, inner conflict. His devotion to his mother and his sense of indebtedness to her, coupled with his own deep sensitivity and his reluctance to hurt anyone, made the tension almost unbearable.

Needless to say, these months were equally traumatic for Irene. Ultimately Joe went to consult Martin Buber who listened to him patiently and then sat with him for a long time in silence. At last he said, quite simply: ''In every decision there is a severing of the deepest tie''. Again they sat in silence until Joe quietly left. Buber did not tell him anything that he did not know but, in the presence of this 'God-possessed' man he received the strength he needed to go forward with the marriage.

Joe and Irene were married in St. George's Cathedral in the presence of a great company of friends — military, missionary, from many church traditions and some from other faiths, joining in what by general consent was an outstandingly joyous occasion.

Joe, who so often lamented the fact that he was unprepared for an important occasion, especially a sermon, behaved in characteristic fashion even on his wedding day. Ian Thomson, his best man, (a friend since Oxford days) dined with him the night before (the day of the marriage August 15 proved to be exactly one year before the end of the War) and then, on the morning itself, found Joe trying to meet a deadline for notes which he had promised to write on the prophet Jeremiah. ''It was touch and go whether he'd make the wedding. Fortunately we only had a few yards to walk to the Cathedral (Joe was living in St. George's Hostel) but I was getting most anxious. Ten minutes before the service I told him to stop writing, handed him a clean handkerchief and his shoes which I had rubbed over, and asked him to put away his notes with the warning that Irene would get there first if we didn't hurry. That did it. We made it. He in Army uniform, me in R.A.F. What I remember most'' Ian concluded ''is the galaxy of representatives of Eastern Churches in the congregation — a tribute to his gift for friendship''.

Ian put the finishing touches to Joe's attire, but even before a small army of willing helpers had made it their happy task to see that Joe, who cared little about his own appearance, looked the part of bridegroom — his clothes had been pressed for him, his brass buttons, buckle, and insignia cleaned, his leather belt and shoes polished till they glittered. That it was nervousness which kept him trying to work to the last minute was proved when, on returning from their honeymoon, the notes on Jeremiah had been returned, with a note to say that the typist was unable to read his handwriting!

It was a special joy to Joe that two friends from Egypt were present, Dr. Marcus Gregory, with whom he had shared so many plans and ideas since they first met in Addis Ababa in 1932, and Harry Gabb, organist of Llandaff Cathedral before the War, and later to become organist of St. Paul's and Master of the Queen's music, whose rendering of Purcell and Bach and Handel would have rejoiced his Aunt Connie's heart if, as Joe wrote her, she had been able to be present. Appropriately the address was about music and the way in which the joining of two musical themes creates a third, more fully developed than could have been the case for either alone.

The service was followed by a reception in the beautiful drawing room of the American Colony, and then Joe and Irene left for their honeymoon. But after two days Joe fell ill of amoebic dysentery, so that it was not an ideal honeymoon, and on returning to Jerusalem he had to spend $3\frac{1}{2}$ weeks in hospital.

After his recovery, Joe and Irene lived, at first in the American Colony, and then occupied the homes of missionaries whilst they were on leave. At the end of July 1945 their first daughter, Carolyn, was brought into the world by an eminent, German trained, Jewish gynaecologist in the Government Hospital, and cared for by Arab, Armenian, Abyssinian and Jewish nurses under an English sister. In England, that day, Mr. Churchill's government was defeated by Labour. Joe was so excited by the birth of his first child that he forgot (probably for the first time in his life) to keep abreast of the news. He declared himself "thrilled", but "totally lost". However, in the next 3 months he mastered the intricacies of caring for a small baby — which was lucky, for Irene caught sunstroke during the fortnight they had to spend in a transit camp in Egypt, waiting for a boat to bring them back to England.

IV

In 1945 the war was drawing to an end and Joe knew that he would not be in the army much longer. He must go *forward,* that was clear. But in what direction? Proposals began to be made to him. What appeared to be a most attractive job in New Zealand was offered for his consideration but somehow he felt it would be in the nature of an escape from the problems of post-war England to which he ought now to return. "I think it would really have been a run-away" he wrote, "and in the long run, if you don't face up to Reality, you are sunk, however far you may appear to go". Again and again he deplored human tendencies to dodge real issues and to escape from real situations. Another suggestion came that he might work in the

University of London, establishing a Pastorate along the same lines as those which existed in Oxford and Cambridge. But in a certain sense this would have been a going back to the kind of situation which he had left behind. His work in Jerusalem amongst those belonging to other traditions and other faiths had been so successful that it is strange that no proposal seems to have been made, then or later, for him to continue to make his contribution somewhere in the Middle East.

Quite unexpectedly an invitation came in the spring of 1945 which seemed to offer the possibility of a new kind of ministry: a settled base and home with, at the same time, freedom to carry on the work of an evangelist by preaching and lecturing and writing. The Bishop of Rochester, Dr. C. M. Chavasse, knew Joe all through his days in Oxford, including his time as curate of St Aldate's where Chavasse had once been Rector. One of the residentiary canonries at Rochester had fallen vacant and he jumped at the possibility of bringing Joe into the Diocese. He commended his name to the Lord Chancellor and the invitation was extended. In April 1945 the decision was made, though it would be more than six months before final demobilisation came and the family could begin the journey homewards to be installed in the large, cold house awaiting them in Rochester. I have already referred to one other significant mile-stone in his life which marked his Palestine experience. It was the completion in Quinquagesima 1944 of his first piece of theological writing, a series of brief and often pungent comments on successive sections of the Gospel of Mark. He made no attempt to deal with questions of literary form or historical provenance but concentrated all his efforts on showing how the Gospel sets forth good news about Jesus.

He chose as his key theme the phrase *The New Order*. He had already indicated that his great hope was that after the war a new England would emerge, a new spirit, a new co-operation, a new vision of what Christianity really means. He often quoted the promise ''I will make all things new'' and in the little book on Mark he tried to show how such a new order was actually inaugurated by Jesus through his words, his actions, his suffering and his death. The Gospel dealt in sequence, he believed, with the preparation, the proclamation, the constitution, the working and the character of the New Order: its clash and conflict with the Old Order: and finally the victory of the New Order through the way of sacrifice and the passion of love. These major themes were destined to emerge again and again in his ministry back in England.

Not only does this little booklet set forth the main themes. It also bears striking witness to the *form* of communicating his message which he would constantly employ. There is no quiet development of an argument, no subtle reasoning such as he was familiar with when studying Greek philosophy. Instead — and here perhaps unconsciously he adhered far more closely to the typical Hebrew pattern — he chose the method of parallelism and contrast. His very first comment on the nature of God's Kingdom reads: "good news not good advice: fact not idea: Person not programme: national not nationalist: universal not particular: for all not for some". More often he turned the contrast the other way round and this was probably even more effective. If the negative comes first the hearers' expectations are aroused to know what the positive will be. There is a moment of suspense and this sustains interest. Particularly in Joe's case, seeing that he could draw on an unusually varied store of adjectives, there was the frequent surprise when he exploded with a word which was sometimes devastating, never tame or merely conventional.

This is his comment on Jesus' word to Peter about building his church on the rock.

"Now He could begin building; and what He would build was the church: not a defensive buttress of morality and of the *status quo* but a battering ram of revolution crashing through the barricades of Hell". The metaphors may be a bit mixed but no one could ever accuse Joe of being *dull* in his use of imagery and language. He loved to quote Jung's dictum: "Creative living is on the yonder side of convention". He would never crush the bruised reed with a word of sarcasm. Equally he was always ready to prick the 'bubbles of self-importance and self-satisfaction' with a verbal barb whose point was inescapable.

7

Pneumatology and Eschatology

The change from Jerusalem to Rochester towards the end of 1945 must have tested Joe's and Irene's powers of adjustment to the limit. From the sunshine and clear air of the city amongst the hills to the clouds and mists of the Medway valley: from a place where there was no lack of essential foods to the restrictions of rationing and queueing: from the richly ecumenical life, both of the churches with ancient traditions and of the varying denominations represented in the army, to the dominating position of the Church of England in cathedral and city: and from the small but manageable quarters in which they had lived with their baby daughter to a vast Canon's house needing repair, re-decorating, more adequate heating and furniture. It was not until Easter 1948 that Joe was able to report that at last they were hoping to get things in order.

Fortunately Irene possessed an eye to see what could be done to make the house habitable and gradually the garden also was brought under control. At least Prior's Gate House, Rochester, provided plenty of room for a growing family. Marianne arrived in March 1947, Flint in April 1949 and David in the year they left Rochester, 1952. Joe loved children but broken nights and pram-pushing were new experiences. At the time of the birth of Marianne, when he was temporarily left to look after Carolyn, he reported to his mother: "Carolyn is still alive under my care. In fact she grows daily and I am quite sure I never did a stroke of work before in my life". He claimed that through his sorties with the pram he came to know every inch of the Rochester High Street. New life had begun at 40.

Canon D. R. Vicary, who was appointed Director of Religious Education in the Rochester Diocese in 1948, has recalled some of the tremors that shook the Cathedral Close when Joe and his family took up residence in it. Their house was opposite the corner of Minor Canon Row where an old Oxford friend, Noel Wardle-Harpur lived. "Noel had a booming voice and he and Joe used to conduct a conversation across the road from the bathroom windows so that one elderly Canon's wife referred to this place as 'Hell-fire Corner'". Joe was the first Canon ever to be seen in corduroy trousers which peeped beneath his cassock. "He was certainly the first dignitary to be seen changing a child's nappy in the precincts".

Canon Selwyn Gummer, another clerical friend, has written: "Joe's love of parenthood was almost comical. It was not that

ERRATA

p.v, l.18 insert "for" between "been" and "me".

p.33, l.15 for "pretense" read "pretence".

p.62, Section 3, l.8 for "furture" read "future".

p.71, l.16 for "unfamilia" read "unfamiliar".

p.73, l.26 for "the" read "they".

p.98, l.27 for "visitior" read "visitor".

p.102, 5 lines from the bottom for "license" read "licence".

p.124, l.5 for "abides" read "asides".

p.124, 6 lines from bottom for "furture" read "future".

p.128, l.9 delete "ailment" and start sentence "It".

p.135, l.3 for "wods" read "words".

We ungraciously omitted to name the cover artist; it is Miss Pamela Franklin.

We know there are other literal errors for which we crave the reader's indulgence.

he thought or hoped that he had fathered a brood of geniuses: it was for him an unbelievable fact that he, Joe Fison, had, by the grace of God, produced anything more than an article for a religious journal or an occasional book. To him the birth of his children far outweighed any literary or scholastic achievement. He stood before them in wonder as he would have done had he been Joseph at Bethlehem 2000 years before.

"In many ways Joe remained a big boy at heart. Never was this more in evidence than at the children's parties which Irene seemed to organise every other week or so (although that could not have been quite the case!) Uncle Joe was the games master and one can see him now on the floor at Prior's Gate with a dozen or so children tumbled on top of him.

"At Rochester family joys and responsibilities became part of Joe's world. In a measure he now lived in two worlds, activities in Cathedral and Diocese and in other parts of England on the one hand, the return for refreshment and renewed awareness of the ordinary simplicities of life within the family circle on the other".

1946-7 brought one of the coldest winters of this century. Carolyn was just over 2 years old and the nearest maternity home, to which Irene went for the birth of Marianne, was in Gravesend, seven miles away. The day before the new baby was born, the girl whom Irene had trained to look after Carolyn, suddenly left to marry a sailor boy-friend. Another girl had agreed to help with housework and cooking but now she and Joe had to be responsible for Carolyn as well. It was bitterly cold and during the two weeks of Irene's absence Joe drove an ancient Vauxhall car, recently acquired, day by day over perilous icy roads to visit her. He had no practical or mechanical abilities of any kind (he once took the car to a garage to have the lights mended only to find that they were covered with mud) but he was an exceptionally good driver. He loved to drive fast and over rough roads. There was a strong streak of competitiveness in his nature: it gave him immense satisfaction to win at games, to reach the highest point of a climb and, I suspect, to pass the other car-driver.

Joe found former students of Wycliffe Hall in the Rochester area with young families like his own and there was plenty of coming and going between the various households. As Prior's Gate House was so large it was possible to entertain guests and even to include a lodger within the family circle. One such who occupied a room in the house during the inside of each week over a period of six months has written of the way he became almost a member of the family, never feeling that he was an imposition on them. "Joe's warm cheerful character made the family a remarkably happy one. I would almost say he was an ideal father". Irene, though by nature more inclined to live quietly with the children, did her best to share Joe's wish to create open house and to make the home a centre of warm hospitality.

Joe's legal obligations at the Cathedral were confined to three month's residence per year. Chapter meetings claimed his attendance but his not infrequent absence caused the Dean on one occasion to remark somewhat wistfully: "Canon Fison, the world is his parish". The Bishop put him in charge of ordinands and recently ordained clergy in the Diocese and in addition he was in great demand for sermons on special occasions, quiet days, lectures at clergy conferences, summer schools, evangelistic missions, prize-givings — there were few parts of England where his voice was not heard, few parishes in the Rochester Diocese where he did not preach. At a time when the country as a whole was engaged in recovering from the austerities and devastations of war, Joe's enthusiasm and freshness of presentation of Biblical themes gained a ready response.

At times an idea or an issue so captivated him that he ran ahead of his audiences and left them bewildered. It is even recorded that one Sunday evening sermon in Rochester produced the very opposite effect to that which he intended and that he had to come again on the following Sunday to put matters right. His experiences abroad had helped to make him uncompromising on race prejudices — Jew and Gentile, black and white. When in 1950 the marriage of Seretse Khama startled conservative circles in Britain, Joe wrote to the press expressing his conviction that the question of mixed marriages must be squarely and fairly faced if there was to be any hope of future world unity. He believed that the early Church had found the way to reconciliation between Jew and Gentile "in Christ". The parallel tension between black and white in the modern world could only be resolved in the same way.

II

When he had established himself in Rochester it was suggested to him that he should give time to writing as well as to preaching and lecturing. First he was asked to consider writing a book on the Holy Spirit and as a result his first volume appeared in 1950 entitled *The Blessing of the Holy Spirit.* His freshness and liveliness of approach gained him a ready hearing as he made the Bible spring to life and related it to modern conditions. His second book, which followed in 1952, was entitled *Understanding the Old Testament* and was directed more particularly to sixth formers or college students needing a clear and engaging introduction to this part of the Bible.

Both of these books sprang out of his own experience. He was deeply convinced that he had himself been guided, inspired, checked, instructed by the Holy Spirit and he was ever eager to bear witness to the work of the Third Person of the Trinity. At the same time he possessed a rich store of memories of the Holy Land, its people and its history and about these he could write vividly. Could he also produce a more substantial theological work which would commend itself to experts in the field of doctrine?

The largest and most scholarly volume from his pen was *The Christian Hope* published in 1954. In this he attempted to examine afresh the Christian views of the future, how God's final purpose would be worked out for nations and for individuals. Then in 1957 his most extensive book on the Bible appeared — a Pelican entitled *The Faith of the Bible* — while a year later he returned to the theme of the Holy Spirit in a small but vigorous piece of writing entitled *Fire on the Earth*. It seems that it was at this point that a major decision had to be taken. Would he try to make further contributions to the Church by means of theological teaching and writing or would he involve himself more fully in action, debate, pastoral concerns, evangelism in the widest sense? He decided for the latter and no more books were written.

What then did he contribute through his writings? Undoubtedly in his treatment of the Old Testament he displayed a lively sympally for Jews and their ancestral faith, together with an obvious affection for the land and the city which figured so largely in their memories and hopes. He fastened upon the adjective *Holy* and used it for some 20 chapter titles — Land, City, Place, Patriarchs, Prophets etc. "The Jews had a name for this God of theirs. They called him the Holy One; and so because he was holy they were a holy nation, and their country was a holy land, their temple was a holy place, and their bible was a holy book". The very choice of *holiness* as his key category involved him in a certain tension for it is impossible to dissociate the original use of the term from separation, apartness, removal from the secular and profane. Yet one of his abiding concerns was to declare that just as Jesus was involved in the secular affairs of the world, so too must all true religion seek identification rather than isolation. In God's providence there had to be a distinctiveness, a particularity, a separation from the general and the ordinary, a land, a city, a temple, a law. But none of these was ever intended to be an end in itself. So he claimed that in Jesus, his life, death, and resurrection, the very idea of holiness was transformed and the holy God came to be known as the Redeemer of all mankind.

In his two books on the Bible he *felt* with his Jewish friends their sense of privilege, their agonies, their longings for the future. Nevertheless he could not minimize what in two major sections of *The Faith of the Bible* he called *The Catholicity of Jesus Christ* and *The Apostolicity of Christianity*. There could be no weakening of the witness to Jesus Christ as universal Saviour and to the responsibility of His followers to go out into all the world. Though he may have had doubts about certain missionary methods, he could never support any system that was exclusive and inturning. The very essence of true life was *meeting*. The Jews, he said, were "not a series of people with bright ideas of their own about God". Rather they were "a series of people who kept on meeting Someone — and they had no doubt he was always the same someone". In and through these meetings, God revealed Himself and prepared the way for the critical and climactic meeting in and through Jesus the Christ.

III

The two books on the Bible may not have contributed anything original to the world of scholarship but they exuded a warmth and an enthusiasm born out of recent personal experience. This commended them to readers without specialist or technical knowledge. His most substantial book, however, *The Christian Hope,* was designed as a new approach to Christian eschatology. For a considerable time he had been gazing into the *furture*. What were the prospects for the victorious allies, for the defeated, for the oppressed in the world, for the individual? He had become vividly aware of the appeal of Marx and of the utopian promises of the communists. What had Christianity to offer as a constructive alternative? What was the true meaning of the term *Parousia* which expressed the hope of the early disciples?

The sub-title of his book is intriguing: *The Presence and the Parousia* Here is another example of that 'creative tension' within which he himself lived and which he tried to advocate as an essential ingredient of Christian living. The Presence he associated with the mystical tradition: the Parousia with the prophetic and eschatological. "A present mysticism to correct a crude future eschatology is as vital as is a future eschatology to correct a vague sentimental''. This polarity he illustrated by a wide ranging examination of the Scriptures and the history of Christianity. In simplest terms it can be said that disciples met the Lord on earth in the days of his incarnation and continue to meet him through his sacramental presence: at the same time they looked forward to meeting the Lord 'in the air', at a time when the divine purpose had been completely fulfilled, and this hope can still be the inspiration of Christians to-day.

The secret of true life, he claimed, is the meeting of persons in the reciprocity of *love*. Commenting on the witness of the Fourth Gospel he wrote: ''St. John realized that the essence of a personal parousia as much as of a personal presence (and in love as much as in etymology the two terms are inseparable) can never be ostentatious. For the meaning of personality is most clearly shown in love and love is always self-effacing. This does not in the least mean that the presence or the parousia of love is subjective rather than objective. It means that persons are most clearly revealed as persons not when they stand in definable objectivity over against each other, nor certainly when they lose their identity and merge it in some undefinable and perhaps disembodied annihilation of each other, but on the contrary when they meet each other in love and in the meeting disclose to each other the secret of their personalities. That is the secret of revelation, for that is the secret of love, which cannot disclose itself in any other way. It is the secret of the embodied sacramental presence as much as of the embodied eschatological parousia. It is in such reciprocal intercourse of love that the meaning of the new dimension of eternal life is disclosed''. (182)

It could be claimed, I think, that the whole book revolves around that which is summarized in this passage. Joe discusses the current situation in the world, the advance of communism, racial barriers, the meaning of history, Messianism, the day of the Lord, the pattern of development in the New Testament, resurrection and immortality, but time and again he returns to the central concept of *lovers meeting*. ''Journeys end in lovers meeting''. This he believed to be at the very heart of Christian experience and Christian hope.

In *The Christian Hope* he tried to weave together the three strands which had come to mean so much to him in thought and experience: pneumatology, embracing freedom and the Spirit: eschatology, embracing freedom and the future: and mysticism, embracing freedom and the sacramental presence. He did not despise or under-estimate the importance of forms and institutions but clung to the conviction that at any time and in

63

any place the transcendent happening might occur — the meeting with God, the free movement of God's Spirit, the manifestation of God's presence. The old and the traditional could be an inspiration and a guide but never a guarantee or an unchangeable norm. 'Behold I make all things *new*'.

Yet it has to be admitted that this book did not make the impact that Joe may have hoped for. It tended to be repetitive, circling again and again around the one central theme. It revealed his wide interests and his catholic tastes in reading but it hardly came to grips with the difficulties that many have come to feel about the future, either for society at large or for the individual. It contains eloquent passages and some of the sparkling comments which one associates with the author but it did not become a definitive work on Christian eschatology. He will be remembered more for his two books on pneumatology in which his eyes were focussed on demands and possibilities within the present situation rather than on the uncertainties and indeterminacies of the future.

IV

The invitation to write a book on the Holy Spirit gave him the chance to declare his own position after some five years absence from the regular life of the Church of England. These five years abroad had been immensely liberating in all kinds of ways and as he reflectecd on the changes that had taken place, he saw them as clear evidences of the working of God's free, holy and life-giving Spirit. He was prepared to celebrate the Third Person in the Holy Trinity as he had come to discern the marks of His working in the life of mankind, both as recorded in the Bible and the history of the Christianity on the one hand, and as seen in the contemporary situation of the post-war world on the other.

In no other of his books was he so outspoken, so hard-hitting, as in *The Blessing of the Holy Spirit*. At first sight if might appear that he spared no one. Yet it is also true that he never tried to spare himself, never criticized with any air of superiority, never swerved from his final aim which was to bear witness to the living God and to the new possibilities of the operation of his Spirit.

His opening sentence threw down a challenge comparable to that which Karl Barth had issued some thirty years earlier. Only, whereas in Barth's case, the clarion call was to a re-discovery or a rehearing of the *Word* of God, in Joe's case it was to a re-discovery or a re-experiencing of the blessing of the *Spirit* of God. "In a religious situation" he declared, "in which liberal protestantism has lost touch with the supernatural, and evangelical pietism and catholic mysticism have lost touch with the natural, the supreme need of the Christian church is a rediscovery of the blessing of the Holy Spirit . . . The characteristic of the Spirit, Who is fully personal and distinctively holy, is self-effacement and not self-advertisement. Hence there is a peculiar danger of the dethronement of the Holy Spirit from the Godhead, and the result is inevitable — idolatry, apostasy or blasphemy.

"The full trinitarian faith stakes all on the fact, vindicated at the Cross, that despite all appearances to the contrary, this universe is both law-abiding and freedom-loving and , above all, reciprocally related. The gateway to the fullness of this trinitarian blessing is holy baptism into the Triune Name. And this means in practice not so much volunteering for the heroic pioneering of the unknown country of the Spirit as facing, in day-to-day loyalty to our vocation, the known and unavoidable cross in all the stark reality with which it confronts us. The price of Pentecost is Calvary".

In this brief introductory outline he revealed some of his deepest convictions and some of the leading characteristics of his own style of writing. The marks of the Spirit: self-effacement, reciprocal relationship, Pentecost's dependence upon the prior enactment of Calvary. The characteristics of his style: the vivid contrast, the polarity of apparent opposition, the yes and the no, the daring use of the language of extremes (idolatry, apostasy, blasphemy), not so much this as that. He was not out to argue a case. Rather he wanted to startle his readers by confronting them with stark alternatives: through the very clash of human contraries a way might be opened for the divine Spirit to enter into the earth-bound situation and eyes might be opened to recognize the advent of the supernatural.

In the book itself he did not hesitate to speak explicitly, naming individuals and organisations as representing evangelical or catholic, liberal or conservative, biblical or ecclesiastical interests. In so doing he often touched on influences which had affected him personally. Yet even when he felt that they strait-jacketed him intellectually he was quick to recognize the devotion and spiritual earnestness which they often displayed. He first took his readers through the Bible in a lively and well-informed way to show how the movements of the Spirit were often inhibited by reversions to a strict legalism. Then come two chapters containing his severest strictures on the perils of idolatry, apostasy and blasphemy. Biblical fundamentalism idolises a book and inhibits the freedom of the Spirit in interpretation and application. Ministerial and ecclesiastical fundamentalism idolises a particular church-order and hinders the Spirit's activity in creating reciprocal relationships.

I doubt if Joe ever set out his ideal for his own future ministry more clearly than when he wrote:

"If we are to avoid both the Scylla of fundamentalism and the Charybdis of apostate rationalism, we shall be driven to seek in the Holy Spirit the secret of our forward way. And He may not be equated in theory with, nor separated in experience from, either scripture or reason. In Him alone does the revelation of Jesus Christ live down the ages, whatever the medium He employs. It is in this true *via media* that we shall find the more excellent way forward. To venture here is indeed to trust in God the Holy Ghost, the Lord and giver of life, and to find the secret that the gospel of the Paraclete reveals within the scriptures themselves, the possibility of complete reformation and reformulation of truth coupled with utter loyalty to the central truth of the gospel itself. To go this way is to go the way of the cross, to abandon the safeguards and signposts of past sight, not in order to overthrow them, but in order to pioneer the path of faith, and so beyond the cross of Calvary to discover the power of Pentecost".

Six years later he returned to the same subject in the last book he wrote. This time there is much less attention to aberrations and apostasies, to idolatries and cultic eccentricities. The very title *Fire upon the Earth* reveals the depth of his feeling but this time it is poured into a more constructive mould. The book shows that he had reached a comprehensive understanding of the varied and complementary ways in which the Spirit has worked and does still work in human affairs. Strikingly he discovered four P's to designate the major forms of this manifestation — the pietist, the prophetic, the priestly and the philosophical. He prefaced these four by a chapter on what he called the primitive Spirit, and in this he dealt with upsurgings from the unconscious which cannot easily be classified. Three final chapters were directed to the Pentecostal, the Pauline Spirit of Unity and the Johannine Paraclete of Love. Thus in the two concluding chapters he drew together the varying manifestations of the Spirit's activity within a unity of reciprocal love.

The fire symbolism, movingly employed by Jesus at a critical point in His own ministry (I came to cast fire upon the earth; And how I wish that it was now kindled) gave him his title and inspired his exposition. Whatever the particular nature of the Spirit's manifesation might be — new insight, encouragement to corporate participation, synthesizing reflection, or simple personal piety — it would be inspired by the 'fire of love'. The manifold qualities of fire have quickened the human imagination from time immemorial and in using it in his book, and often in his public utterances, Joe stood in a noble succession. He was himself a man of fire, his lips touched by the live coal from off the altar. Yet it was never the fire of destruction, except when he was inveighing against some perversity or outrage. Normally it was the fire of a sympathetic heart and spirit, seeking to draw others into the warmth of its embrace.

This little book is neither a theological treatise nor even a Christian apologia. It is rather the deeply-felt testimony of a man who believed that creative movements and relationships which had influenced his own life and which he had seen operating in the wider life of society must be attributed to a supernatural personal agent, the agent who through long centuries had been known as the Holy Spirit. Like Pascal, whose experience fascinated him, he felt that the coming of the Spirit could best be likened to the refining and consuming and comforting actions of fire. Yet, as T.S. Eliot proclaimed, however fierce the torment, however acute the tension,

Love is the unfamiliar Name

Behind the hands that wove

The intolerable shirt of flame.

Joe had no doubt that his final word must be that the fire of the Spirit is the fire of Love. In that conviction he tried to live: with that as his message he tried to carry on his ministry of reconciliation.

8

Halcyon Days in Cornwall

I

In the summer of 1952 Joe was invited to become Canon Residentiary and Sub-Dean of Truro Cathedral. Some years afterwards (in 1964) he recalled his earliest reactions to this possible change:

"I shall never forget the moment of truth that came to me when a parson in Kent said to me on a point of difficulty "Don't worry about your reasons. Ask yourself what is the motive for your reasons". And I went down to Truro where I was offered a job and as I walked down Tydell St. (and I remember it as clearly as if it was yesterday) I was saying "This is no job". I was saying this to my wife and the baby heard it, although the baby didn't understand. And it came suddenly: there bobbed out to me "Oh you don't want to go there, you have already risen a rung or two in the rank of one ancient cathedral and don't fancy starting at the bottom again. Miserable motive! Concealed behind excellent reasons, the Devil. That's how it always is. That is why we talk about the wiles of the Devil". However the Devil was put firmly in his place and the offer was accepted.

The period during which the parents and their four children (Carolyn 7, Marianne $5\frac{1}{2}$, Flint $3\frac{1}{2}$ and David 6 months) lived in Truro provided the fullest and in many respects the happiest experience of united family life for the Fisons. The general atmosphere of city and cathedral was relaxed, the worst of war-time restrictions had come to an end, there were friends with young families like their own and there was the lovely countryside of Cornwall to explore. Irene identified herself with the Young Wives' Fellowship and under her inspiration the branch flourished. Joe, now responsible for the parish attached to the Cathedral, found full scope for the exercise of his pastoral ministry: the parish became in a remarkable way an extension of his own family.

At the beginning Irene found herself involved in unexpected problems with the house which had been bought for the Sub-Dean. Just as she and the children were moving in (Joe having remained at Rochester to fulfil some final commitments) extensive dry rot was discovered in the floor and this meant six weeks of walking on planks. Then an extension to the house (which seemed necessary for the accommodation of a large family) was ruled out by the Church Commissioners. However these problems were soon alleviated by the kindness of new Cornish friends and Joe was able to see more of the children and to join in more of their activities than would ever be possible later.

He proved to be a born story-teller and, particularly at meal-times, entertained the children by a continuing series about fictional happenings in their own lives. He coined names for himself and them as they appeared in the stories. He was 'The old crock': Carolyn and Marianne 'The scraggly ones': Flint 'The raucous one': and David 'The circular object'. If a friend came to a meal, a suitable nickname would be invented for inclusion in the story.

He loved to play with the children but found it less easy to exercise parental discipline. He would never inflict corporal punishment and when there was quarreling or complaining his usual strategy was to inject some humorous diversion or to rally the disaffected ones round some positive enterprise. Just occasionally he was asked to talk seriously to one of the children about some misdemeanour and the effect then was simply to reduce the offender to unhappy silence. He was not very good either at helping with home work, finding it hard to understand what the child's difficulties of comprehension really were. Yet he never made anyone feel small nor did he ever talk down to some one who did not possess his own intellectual background. His constant ambition was to 'look up' to the neighbour, whatever the age or status of that neighbour might be.

Before his own children were born Joe had a god-daughter Mary (born in 1936) who remembers him as 'superb' in his relationship to her, writing her marvellous letters at Christmas and for her birthday and bringing back presents from Palestine when he returned from the War. When the time came for her to train as a nurse in London, Joe would meet her from time to time and gave her memorable assistance both in re-thinking matters of faith and in deciding about her future profession. A nephew, too, and children of friends, found themselves completely at ease with him and responded at once to his friendly approach. The son of a fellow Canon at Truro looked back to the Lemon House parties which he always enjoyed but which were tinged with some disappointment if Uncle Joe was not present. "It seemed that the whole house and household were much jollier by his presence and distinctly incomplete (as it seemed to a very small boy) without him. Looking back now I also realise that he welcomed me and took me seriously in my own right as a person and not just as one of my parents' children". Irene organised all practical details for children's parties with meticulous care: Joe came in to create excitement and fun and to ensure that there was never a dull moment.

I have said that the parish became an extension of Joe's family. His loud but friendly voice, his obvious interest in the other person, his explosions into laughter seemed able to pierce through any reserve, and soon the Cornish people loved him for they knew that he loved them. There was no limit to what he would do for anyone in trouble, especially for the sick. Hospital visits are never easy but Joe seemed able to put patients at their ease and to bring them just the encouragement they needed.

I give one example, recounted by Henry Lloyd, the first Dean of Truro. It tells how Joe, who was then Bishop of Salisbury, found an opportunity to journey down to Truro to visit an old friend then in hospital.

"I remember one afternoon visiting Henry Southeard in the city hospital. He was a retired craftsman, a great campanologist and churchwarden of St. Mary's parish. Above all he was a modest and unassuming man. I sat by his bed talking with him when suddenly the tired and strained expressions of pain on his face gave way to a look of sheer delight. I realised that he was gazing over my shoulder. I turned and looking down the long ward saw the unmistakable figure of Joe Fison standing in the door way. As he approached the bed he said, "I found I had a free day for once and felt I must come to see my old friend Henry Southeard". I quietly slipped away marvelling that a hard pressed Bishop of Salisbury having a rare free day should spend it driving all the way to Truro to comfort one of his old parishioners as he lay dying. I shall always treasure that little incident as a superb example of unaffected loving pastoral care and the joy and comfort it brought to an old Cornishman — at the ending of his life. I especially recall this occasion because it was so typical of Joe's completely natural and unselfconscious kindness; it was in fact for me one of the nicest and most authentic pastoral acts I have seen because Joe's presence seemed to bring sunshine into that long old fashioned ward. You might say it was the Light of Christ".

II

Joe was invited to Truro to fulfil a particular mission. The Bishop, Dr. E. R. Morgan, combined a wide missionary and ecumenical sympathy with a firm loyalty to Catholic forms of worship and spirituality. He assumed office at Truro in 1951 at a time when there were considerable tensions and differences of opinion in the diocese following on the episcopates of two very distinguished men, Walter Frère, an Anglo-Catholic liturgiologist and Joseph Hunkin, a Liberal Evangelical Biblical scholar. Morgan faced the task of reconciler and as he was himself Dean of the Cathedral it was particularly important to find a sub-Dean who would support him in his efforts to establish a spirit of harmony in the central church of the diocese.

The post might not have been Joe's first choice but he had begun to feel that he ought to move from Rochester.

For more than 10 years life had been exceedingly hectic for him, travelling from place to place, living under war conditions, marrying and beginning a family, struggling in Rochester with post-war austerities and a difficult house not far from busy London. The move to Cornwall gave him the opportunity to think and to write and to gain a new appreciation of hitherto unfamiliar aspects of the Christian tradition; it certainly allowed Irene a chance to establish a more distinctive role in the life of the home and of the community. Moreover Bishop Morgan's hopes for a man who would bring a reconciling spirit were abundantly realised. In a quite remarkable way Joe could sail into a situation where there was suspicion or resentment or a virtually closed mind and almost at once by his own openness and gaiety and unexpected witticisms break down barriers and establish a mutual trust. He could never accept any kind of authoritarian dogma or rigid ecclesiastical system but he came more and more to appreciate the value of traditional Catholic symbolic forms as well as the sense of mystery and wonder displayed in the writings of Catholic mystics. In an article describing one of his first journeys to Cornwall he referred to the impact made on his spirit by stopping off at Avebury and Glastonbury before reaching "the land of the holy wells and of the Celtic crosses and above all of the Cornish saints — we have more than 20 of them commemorated here in the stalls of Truro Cathedral — St. Piran, St. German, St. Petroc, St. Merindoc, St. Ia and all the rest — names I had never heard before I came here". He went on to speak of the mystery of the Kingdom of God, of the need to enter as little children and capture afresh the magic and the romance and the wonder of it all. It was a new world — a world of granite and heather, of headlands and coves, of strange mounds and ancient mines, — with, at its centre, the county town of Truro with its imposing 19th. century Cathedral, erected on a site where Christian worship had been carried on without ceasing over many centuries. He soon felt at home in the cathedral and amongst the people of the parish and enjoyed the more pastoral ministry in which he was now involved.

However it was not all plain sailing. In August 1953 there came a recurrence of the severe internal pains which had troubled him several times before. It seemed evident that he was seriously ill; X-rays revealed that one kidney would have to be taken away and the stone removed from the other (which implied that he might be in poor health for the rest of his life). The news swept round the country with the result that hundreds began to pray for his recovery.

The rest of the story reads like a romance. In Cairo Joe had established a close friendship with Mr. Andrew Logan, subsequently a leading heart surgeon in Edinburgh. He insisted that Joe should come up to the hospital in that city possessing the very latest equipment. There other internal examinations were made and to everyone's amazement the stone, in the kidney which was to have been taken away, began to move. The kidney itself began to function again and it was now possible to crush the stone. But the problem of the other kidney still remained and it was decided that after a week of recuperation Joe would have to re-enter hospital for a major operation.

Irene had so far been with him but at the end of the week was compelled to return for important matters concerning the children, only to find a mysterious telegram awaiting her "Arriving in time for wedding (at which his elder daughter was to be bridesmaid). Love, Joe". It turned out that a final examination of the many X-rays taken suggested to the surgeon that what had been thought to be a stone was probably only a mark on the outer surface of the kidney and of no consequence. This reading was confirmed by his collegues and the patient was told he was free to go. So he returned home to a wedding and general thanksgiving, feeling as he said, a fraud for all the fuss his illness had caused yet wonderfully delivered from what threatened to be a permanent impairment of his health.

III

If the stones caused him bodily pain, developments in the Middle East in 1956 brought him increasing mental anguish. He had lived for long periods in Egypt and in Israel. he had friends in both camps. When the crisis deepened and war broke out he was shattered, being convinced that the British Government had made a fatal mistake. When a meeting was organised in Truro on non-party lines in protest against the policy which was being followed, he agreed to be one of the speakers: though this was far from easy it would have been cowardice, he wrote, to do otherwise.

He regarded the British intervention as the climax of a series of blunders made by both Tory and Labour governments. He did not seek to apportion blame but rather pleaded for a change of policy without delay. In the First World War the British Government made promises to both Jews and Arabs which appeared to them irreconcilable and the breach had never been healed: he believed that there was no justification for the application of force on the part of Israel, understandable though their aggression had been. Now was the time, he urged, for pity not hatred, pity for the Jews forced into a ghetto-like existence, pity for the people of Egypt with their shockingly low standard of living. Only by renouncing our policy of going in alone and by yielding to the demand of the U.N. Council could we, the British, purge our conscience and pursue the things belonging to the peace of the world.

These were the outstanding moments of crisis in domestic and community life in the Truro period. In the wider world Joe made his first broadcast in March 1954 and thereafter was called upon for a series of peoples' services on the radio. He either led or took part in a number of University missions and had the distinction of being the first Anglican to be invited to lecture at the ecumenical institute in Bossey. Irene was able to accompany him and as he was only required to lecture one day each week during the month the visit constituted for them a second honeymoon. The were warmly welcomed and given freedom to attend other lectures at the institute but as these were normally in French or German they took the opportunity to see as much as possible of the beauties of Switzerland.

They had just bought their first *new* car, and so, for three of four days each week, Joe showed Irene some of the loveliest parts of the country. One time they invited an American lecturer and his wife to join them, and set off south of Lake Geneva to Chamonix for a view of Mont Blanc. The plan after that was to drive east and then north over the Grimsel Pass, to Interlaken, and the next day take the cog-wheel train from Grindelwald to the top of Jungfraujoch, 9,473 feet above Interlaken. But there had been an unusually heavy early fall of snow, and in Brig, the last village before the beginning of the pass, they were told that it was impassable. Very disappointed, Joe and the guest would have turned back, but Irene urged them on. She has written: ''Ten miles further, there were large notices stating that the pass was closed. As they halted, they saw a tiny car coming down the pass, and when it reached them, learned that the military had just cleared the road. Joe was a skilful driver, and the new car went well, though parts of the road were very steep and slippery. The next day dawned clear and bright with not a cloud anywhere to mar the amazing journey into a glorious white world glittering in the sunshine, or the incomparable panorama from the top of Jungfraujoch — the 13,640 ft peak of the Jungfrau to the South-west, the Munch and the Eiger to the north and the 10 miles long Aletsch glacier. This shared experience seemed to have a mystical quality for them both which never faded . . .''

Nowhere perhaps did he receive so enthusiastic a reception as he did at the Aberdeen Kirk Week. Few people in Scotland had heard of him and hardly anticipated any explosive utterance from an episcopalian Canon. But Joe was in the land of the great George Adam Smith whose books on the prophets had held him in thrall and by choosing to lecture on the book of Exodus he was able to celebrate Moses as a pioneer in the prophetic succession. His exposition of the story of the burning bush captivated his audience. He relayed something of what he had learned from Martin Buber about the significance of the divine name, doing it with all the dramatic vividness which he so often displayed out of a pulpit and away from a loud-speaker. The Authorised Version ''I am that I am'' became a shout of revelation, ''I am He''. Those involved in Kirk Week took him to their hearts and to his surprise the University of Aberdeen later recognized his contributions to Biblical scholarship by awarding him an honorary doctorate.

Though he often recounted the story of the Bush, he never failed to convey his own sense of wonder as he imagined himself standing alongside Moses. Perhaps above all else he wanted to share this sense of wonder with others so that they might experience it for themselves. In 1957, not long before leaving Truro, he conducted a Mission week in the University of Bristol. The opening words of his inaugural sermon were;

''*The wonder of the search* is the wonder of eternal youth, of those who become like little children, and who because they know, know how little they know. Jesus' parables in Matthew are all about this thrilling search''. Having illustrated the search to-day by examples from different parts of the world, he moved on to an even greater wonder — *the wonder of being sought.* Here came his opportunity to press home his oft-repeated conviction: ''to take up a cross of our own choice is not nearly so important as not to dodge the cross put in our path by God''. It is there that God is searching for us.

But what of *the wonder of finding and of being found?* Conscious awareness of the wonder of God, he affirmed, ''depends on our willingness to do three things''.

(a) We have to face facts, especially those of the natural order.

(b) We have to obey signs, especially of the social order.

(c) We have to explore the meaning of symbols especially those pointing to ultimate reality.

For him the continuing search was the very spice of life. The moment of finding and being found were its peak experiences.

The concluded emphasis on symbols is significant. In earlier years Joe had been an evangelist of the *Word,* devoted to the Gospel and its communication through speaking and writing. But his visit to Bossey in Switzerland and, on the way back to England, to Taizé in France, seemed to arouse in him a far heightened sense of the importance of symbolic forms in worship. He came to recognize in a new way the influence of psychological and aesthetic factors in religion and, on returning from Bossey, wrote an article in which he severely questioned the adequacy of any worship service which could spend 50 minutes on sermon and reading without any attention to ritual and liturgical forms, to symbols or the communion of Saints. After lecturing on worship he felt the more keenly how much the ecumenical church needed the contribution of the Anglican communion but ''not if it either sticks to 1662 and all that, or abandons totally 1662 and all that''. He never ceased to be an evangelist but from this time onwards he tried to appreciate more fully the traditions of Catholic sacramentalism and mysticism and to ally himself with movements (such as that of the community at Taizé) towards a deeper understanding of the place of symbolic forms in Christian witness and worship.

In April 1958 he was invited to consider the possibility of moving almost diagonally across England to become Chancellor of Lincoln Cathedral. This involved him in a real dilemma. At the Truro end certain organisational changes had been taking place and he felt it was time to think of moving. It had been officially decided that the Diocese ought now to have both Bishop and Dean and that when the office of Sub-Dean next fell vacant, a Dean would be appointed. This, when it happened, would enable Bishop Morgan to concentrate on the Diocese. When therefore the Lincoln offer came, it seemed that a possible solution had been found. Joe would have a close association with the Theological College, though he did not relish the prospect of organising adult education throughout the Diocese. Moreover, the Chancellor's house was sorely in need of modernisation. It was agreed that this should be done but it would take many months to complete. The most serious thing was that Joe, though feeling he ought to move, could gain no inner conviction that the job at Lincoln was the right one for him.

However he formally accepted the appointment and arrangements were being made for the Installation when an utterly unexpected new challenge was presented to him. Mervyn Stockwood, under whose leadership the University Church of Great St. Mary's had become a power-house of the religious life of Cambridge, was appointed Bishop of Southwark and the Crown had the responsibility of choosing a successor. Where was the man who could carry forward the kind of ministry which Stockwood had so successfully set in motion? Joe had become known for his enthusiasm, his ability to appeal to students, his ecumenical interests, his biblical scholarship and his lively preaching. He was now informed that the Archbishops and the Bishop of Lincoln had been consulted and all had agreed that he was the man for Cambridge in spite of his promise already given to Lincoln. From this he could honourably withdraw.

Joe found it desperately hard to (as he felt) let Lincoln down. It was several weeks before he was able to give an affirmative answer to the Crown's invitation. Probably he only did so because of the fact that all along he had lacked the inner conviction that he ought to go to Lincoln, even though circumstances both at Truro and at Lincoln seemed to point in that direction. His final decision caused misunderstanding and subjected him to some criticism. He was deeply sorry about it but the die had been cast. Early in 1959 the family moved to Cambridge, Irene facing the new prospect with a heavy heart. She tried never to influence Joe's decisions but it was terribly hard to say good-bye to home and friends in Cornwall. Happily she was nearly as reluctant to leave Cambridge 4 years later.

9

Town and Gown

The university churches at Oxford and Cambridge — St. Mary's at Oxford, Great St. Mary's at Cambridge — occupy strategic positions and possess illustrious traditions. Nearly every one of note in the Church of England over the past four centuries has preached from one or other of their pulpits and some of these sermons have exercised a notable influence upon the development of religious life in Enland. In addition to its role as the church for official university functions, each has been a parish church with responsibility for a small section of the town's population, while Great St. Mary's is also the city church in Cambridge.

Until this century the Vicars of the two churches made arrangements for statutory and special services and performed pastoral duties for their respective flocks. They did not feel called upon to minister to the undergraduate population. College Chapels and churches representing particular ecclesiastical traditions, actively catered for their spiritual needs. But in the 1920's F. R. Barry, when appointed Vicar of St. Mary's, Oxford, envisaged a different role for the university Church and consequently, in the period between the wars, this church became a centre to which undergraduates flocked on late Sunday evenings during term to hear addresses by distinguished men from all over Britain. Further the town congregation began to expand in numbers as people from a wider area in the city found in St. Mary's a congenial programme of worship and instruction in the faith.

No such change, however, took place at Great St. Mary's in Cambridge until the mid 1950's. Then, however, the appointment of Mervyn Stockwood as Vicar in 1955 initiated what has been called a 'revolution'. The new incumbent had become a celebrity in the city of Bristol by reason of his outstanding gifts as pastor and preacher, these being exercised in a crusading spirit ecumenically, socially and politically. He knew how to use the newly available media of communication and was prepared to speak out fearlessly on public issues. Moreover he had come to know personally leaders of society outside the narrow circle of ecclesiastical life.

He immediately set to work to make Great St. Mary's a lively centre both for new experiments in worship and for new exposures to the challenges of the comtemporary world. He invited men and women who had made a mark in social or international affairs to speak from the Church pulpit on Sunday evenings and began also to build up the congregation of regular worshippers. It has been a feature of university life, at least in this century, that it seems subject to a kind of rhythm of ebb and flow so far as religious interest and churchgoing is concerned. For whatever reasons, the mid 1950's was a boom period and Mervyn Stockwood took full advantage of it. Great St. Mary's soon became a centre for eucharistic worship on Sunday mornings and a focus of attraction for undergraduates in particular on Sunday evenings. Both in name and in reality it could be regarded as *the* university church.

However, Mervyn was not destined to remain long in Cambridge. After four years, his reputation as a dynamic leader in social welfare and reform marked him out as the obvious choice for the vacant see of Southwark with all its many problems on the South Bank of the Thames. Who now could maintain the vision and vitality which had characterised his work at Great St. Mary's and at the same time reveal the capacity to adapt to ever changing circumstances, a quality so essential within a university context?

II

In many ways Joe's appointment to the living was a surprise. He was older than Mervyn and had been away from university life for more than 20 years. Whereas Mervyn stood within a liberal Catholic tradition. Joe's background was strongly Evangelical. Mervyn had for a long time been deeply concerned about the Church's responsibilities in the fields of industry and commerce whereas Joe had been the travelling evangelist, not indifferent to social problems but directing his attention primarily to individuals and their personal needs. Was Joe resilient enough, sufficiently up-to-date to appeal to undergraduates and to undertake the pastoral care of what was now a substantial congregation? So far he had never been in a position where the organising of services, the choosing of visiting preachers, the overseeing of buildings and finance had been his own special responsibility. Moreover it might not be easy for an Oxford man to relate himself quickly to the different atmosphere and traditions of the Cambridge scene.

Whatever qualms of this kind may have been in people's minds were quickly dispelled. Having made the critical decision to withdraw from the Lincoln prospect and thereby to abandon any hope of engaging in theological lecturing and writing, Joe entered on his new task with an almost boyish enthusiasm. He had during the past 20 years travelled widely and was deeply interested in the changes which were taking place all over the world. His eyes were constantly set towards the future and now he was to be in daily contact with young men and women preparing to take their part in that future. Above all he loved individuals and was eager to relate himself to the members of Great St. Mary's regular congregation as well as to the scores of undergraduates who came his way. He expressed publicly his deep indebtedness to his predecessor and the general pattern of activities at the church remained unchanged. Yet, as always, Joe was his inimitable self and soon his presence and his words from the pulpit were making a deep impression. As one of his congregation later put it, when it was known that he would soon be leaving Cambridge, his "sermons and readings of Scripture, his Bible study classes and talks to Young Wives have always spoken directly to my condition and been of immeasurable help".

As far as the family were concerned the children saw much less of him than at Truro. Boarding-schools began to take them away in term-time and in their vacations Joe was often engaged at the Church. Still he remained deeply attached to them and welcomed every opportunity to enter into discussions with them about social and international problems. He had an intense interest in what was going on in the wider world and talked to them about incidents far away as if they were happening in the next street.

As the children developed he never dreamed of forcing his opinions on them or of pressing them to proceed in a particular direction. Neither of the boys was urged to choose Oxford rather than Cambridge or to adopt a vocation to the ministry. After school days were finished the girls were allowed to travel on their own to different parts of the world if they so wished. He was old fashioned about boy friends, thinking that any demonstration of affection indicated that an engagement to marriage was imminent. But again he did not try to influence decisions even when, as in the case of Carolyn, the partner proved to be a member of another faith.

It is impossible for a casual visitor to gain more than a superficial impression of what goes on in regular family life and I therefore quote some of the memories of Joe's elder son, Flint, looking back in particular at his own years of adolescence.

"The impression of his outward personality that comes to me, and I dare suggest was what I experienced, was that of a sincere and born actor whose talents were the boisterous and the affectionate touch. He came over to me and influenced me more by this display than by person to person coversation which

79

I always prized but which he was always shirking. Maybe he lacked confidence in worldly affairs and the involvments of personal relations and educative development and had the integrity to avoid normal talk in these spheres, and maybe he judged me rightly to be not mature enough for discussion of the intellectual and spiritual studies and wisdom which were his wavelength. Maybe it was the way he was brought up and he was unsure of how to talk seriously to a youngster and adolescent who had not been educated, as I think he may have been, to behave and speak like a self-possessed grown-up. Anyway I was weak at making friends or even acquaintances and on a number of occasions he said he felt I had inherited this from him. As well as my serious conversation with my father being limited I cannot remember being present when his conversation with other members of the family as a group or individually, or with friends or acquaintances, became really involved and engaged, as opposed to affectionate appreciation of them or their friends and families or reminiscences or the friendly swapping of intellectual interests.''

In April 1960, at the end of his first year as Vicar, he talked with a reporter from the undergraduate paper *Varsity* about his work. First he described his responsibilities to the Town congregation. ''There has been progress in the past year. Communicants are up: collections are up: a rather unpopular Church Membership Campaign has been successfully carried through and we are making a start with youth work. But what does all this add up to? We are hardly touching the teen-agers, we haven't got any children's work, and we haven't got any premises for parish socials, youth club or children's work. The vicar has no private study to see people in, the church has hardly any social amenities and we depend on Market Hill for our toilets.

''This will not do.

''Therefore I hope that after this summer's redecoration and restoration of the nave and external battlements and the overhaul of both church organs we shall proceed with two large, costly, but quite necessary tasks. (i) The building of a proper block of vestries with toilet accomodation under the West Tower . . . (ii) the complete overhaul of St. Michael's (a redundant church only a few yards away) and its re-creation as a centre of church work''.

This extract reveals a side of Joe's ministry which has not often been recognized. It is true that he was primarily a prophet and evangelist but in addition he was successful in carrying through a programme of re-construction and re-ordering both in the west end of Great St. Mary's and also in St. Michael's. These new facilities have been of inestimable service to the clergy and people of the parish. The re-creation of St. Michael's (in which he had the help of the brilliant imagination of the church-architect Mr. George Pace) provided what can be regarded as a worthy outward memorial of his busy years in Cambridge.

In the interview he then looked at the undergraduate situation. "The university church should not attempt to do for undergraduates what only their college chapels can possibly do: we can only supplement the work of the chapels". This supplement was being provided through the late Sunday evening addresses by those known to be expert in some particular field. In addition he hoped to develop more opportunities for the consideration of philosophical issues: "religion ought not to be a department of life but the way we look at all life": of ethical issues — what are the practical implications to-day of the traditional concern for poverty, chastity and obedience? of the nature of personal prayer and 'exciting' Bible Study and of the call to life-long vocations in Christian service. He concluded the interview by referring to the church's ministry to 'agnostics', the continuation of what Mervyn Stockwood had tried to do for 'fringers'.

"There is certainly a great interest in religion in Cambridge. I am not so sure about the Easter faith. Reverent agnosticism may be enough to describe the spirit of Nicodemus who performed the last rites on Jesus' dead body; it is entirely inadequate to describe the bewilderment of the first visitors to the Empty Tomb.

"It is the agonised bewilderment that I feel Cambridge lacks.

"And notice what caused the bewilderment — a fact, new, unexpected, unprecedented, and for which there was no accounting. Surely there are such new facts constantly facing undergraduates. But where is there evidence of their utter bewilderment?

"It is only out of this bewilderment that wonder comes and with wonder faith as the explanation of the strange new fact begins to dawn".

Finally he summarized his opinion of religion in Cambridge as one needing *bewilderment* in face of inescapable facts, *costly decision* in the light of available evidence and *confidence* born out of these experiences. Joe himself returned again and again in imagination to the Burning Bush and the visions of the Risen Lord. Whatever subjects of current interest might be brought before audiences in Great St. Mary's, his ultimate hope was that out of bewilderment hearers would awaken to wonder and to faith.

III

Life at Cambridge proved to be far more hectic than had been the case at Truro. There was the constant journeying to and fro from the Vicarage on Madingley Road to the Church at the centre of town. There was the constant entertainment of visiting preachers and lecturers. Events had to be planned long in advance and the feverish activities of term-time slackened off only to a degree in vacations: Joe took his pastoral responsibility to the regular congregation very seriously.

Fortunately Irene was there to support him and to maintain the organisation of the home-situation. Joe seemed to have little awareness of money problems and depended largely on Irene to organise family finances. Nor did he pay much attention to dress though he was never untidy. But he saw little need of new clothes for himself though others won his approval when they were well-dressed. As an Evangelical he had been used to simple cassock and surplice in church and with these it was impossible to go far wrong. But when it came to wearing eucharistic vestments he often seemed ill at ease and unable to adjust them properly. Still later, cope and mitre frequently went askew.

Yet Irene had her moments of frustration. Some members of Great St. Mary's congregation admired her skill in designing new hats and were vastly amused when they learned that Joe, returning one evening to the Vicarage, saw a large package on the floor which he imagined was for disposal. Sweeping it up in his arms he carried it off to the Church's jumble sale. In fact Irene had been suddenly called upstairs and had left on the floor her material for the construction of hats. Joe's impulsiveness and his very frailties endeared him to his parishioners. There was no hesitancy or standing on ceremony. As a young visitor to the home put it: "When he went out to anyone with a word or gesture, his whole being went with it. He gave people importance by concentrating on them without consideration of self-regard, social status etc." There was no need to wait to discover what mood Joe was in or what the pressure of business might be. Your presence was his pleasure, your concern his concern. In the home there was no attempt to hide feelings and put on a show of welcome. The welcome was straightforward and uninhibited.

IV

In 1960, Joe preached twice on the second Sunday in October at the beginning of Michaelmas Term. In the morning it was the occasion of Harvest Festival at Great St. Mary's and the title of the sermon was *Man or Beast?* At the beginning of a new academic year it was, he urged, a supreme chance to see things from a new *perspective* and to this end nothing could be more appropriate than Teilhard de Chardin's recently published book, *The Phenomenon of Man.* However much man may have in common with the beast he is distinct in that he is made 'in the image of God' and therefore has the capacity to *create:* he can also *communicate* with his fellows, a two-way process demanding learning not only of his own language but also of that of others.

Teilhard had provided a new perspective. But man is subject to *perils.* Prominent among these — something Joe never ceased to emphasize — is that of *willed isolation,* escapism whether by an individual or by a society. During his period at Great St. Mary's the question of entry into the Common Market had become a burning issue. In a passionate address on the subject, while disclaiming any special knowledge concerning the political and economic aspects, he declared his own belief that' spiritually and morally, closer integration of Britian with the rest of Europe was vitally important. Dismissing fears of betrayal whether of our past, our friends, our independence or our way of life, he went on to give theological reasons in support of a readiness to join the E.E.C. ''The Christian religion is committed to a life in relationship: Intercourse, Conversation and Cross Fertilisation. (He had seen the results of this in nature during his time in Cornwall) . . . In the past years we have been helped by cross fertilization, not with Commonwealth except for the non-British parts of it e.g. South India — but with Europe. Biblically, despite all perils, we owe so much to Germany; theologically, to Germany and Switzerland; liturgically, to Germany, Austria and France; ministerially, to France; evangelistically, to France. These are the things that have thrilled us and kindled our imagination: Barth, Taizé, Priest-Workmen, the Liturgical movement, Ronchamp etc: and they almost all come from the Common Market countries!

''The Christian religion is committed to the *Principle of the Incarnation,* facing life as it is and accepting it as the first condition of doing anything about it. But we are sheltered from so much of life as it is, in this island. If we went into Europe we should be confronted with its starker realities. We need to be in

Europe to realise their implications if we are to maintain any semblance of our way of life.

"The Christian religion is committed to a life of *Hope in the Future*. Of course this hope must be in God. But this country needs some proximate national hope to live and work for, as well as an ultimate spiritual hope. I believe a vision of a common service to the whole world *through Europe* might give us back the best of the old hope of service to the world through the Empire".

After the perspective and the perils the *possibilities:* to work, to co-operate with his fellows, and still to depend utterly on God. Nor only for the harvest of the natural world but also for things spiritual. "I planted, Apollos watered, but God gave the increase".

After speaking in the morning about man's position and potentialities in the created order, Joe preached in the evening the first of a series of addresses arranged for the term on a subject very near to his own heart — *The Wind of Change*, a title recently made famous by its application to Africa by Harold Macmillan. As a motto to preface the series he chose a sentence which often appeared in his public utterances and which he owed to the Provost of his Oxford College, Canon B. H. Streeter: "Only when the ship is in motion does the helm guide". This he believed with all his heart. It was his own vocation as a prophet to discern what were the significant changes taking place in the world around and how through them God was guiding mankind forward in the accomplishing of his purpose.

Looking back now it is possible to see that there was some kind of turning-point in the cultural life of the Western world around the year 1960. It was not only in Africa that the wind of change was blowing but also in Britain and particularly amongst the generation that was then coming to the age of self-confidence and self-expression. Probably the major instrument effecting this rapid change was the television set which in Britian was just then finding a place in vast numbers of homes. New life-styles, new patterns of behaviour, new dress-fashions, new musical rhythms could be rapidly disseminated. The destruction and austerities associated with World War II were a thing of the past and, although there was the background threat of nuclear warfare, the young were determined to make their voices heard and to break out into new freedoms while opportunities lasted.

To a considerable degree Joe shared these new aspirations, for he himself had struggled to break free from inhibiting constraints and so had adopted as his slogan 'Freedom and the Future'. He had kept close to young people and sympathised with their desires for emancipation. So in the first of the series on *The Wind of Change* he began by drawing vivid word-pictures of the ship which is more likely to be destroyed by hugging the shore than by courageously facing the storm in the open sea and of the peoples who established the earliest known civilisation in the Nile Delta by leaving their familiar habitat and accepting the challenge of a new area and a new pattern of life. Then, characteristically, he declared "God is not becalmed". (Probably a dramatic raising of the voice at this point!) He is on the move, as the prophet Ezekiel discerned and symbolised in the 'mysterious and thrilling manoeuvres' of the wheels. We who are made in God's image must be on the move too.

He then turned to life in Cambridge at the beginning of a new academic year. To those in their first term the dominant impression must be that of the *whirl* of endless attractions and possibilities for broadening the mind: the way forward was that of plunging in, finding one's own bent and making the most of available opportunities. Yet there was the danger of being sucked down into what he called the *vortex* of Cambridge life — social or intellectual or athletic or sexual — any pursuit made the instrument for pandering to self-justification. The constructive alternative was to be found by starting on the upward path of the *spiral* of Cambridge life. Inevitably we all go round and round as we fulfil our daily duties but it is possible also to climb. And climbing is never easy: in one way or another it means the way of the Cross.

I have summarized these two sermons for they seem to me to typify the kind of ministry that Joe exercised in Cambridge. He felt a deep responsibility for his regular congregation and tried to provide for their spiritual needs by promoting truly corporate worship and by relating the witness of the Bible to their contemporary problems. He made himself available for pastoral counselling and by his outgoing friendliness gained a firm place in their affections.

In relation to undergraduates he tried constantly to sense the public issues which interested them and at the same time to give guidance on the more personal problems which come to most students in the course of thier university careers. He did not seek the sensational but he never shrank from saying the sharp and challenging word when he felt it was needed. It was always said however within the wider context of that infectious *joie de vivre* which emanated from him. There was never a trace of pomposity or self-righteousness, attitudes peculiarly offensive to those feeling their way to their own independence. He got alongside them and broke down barriers by some shaft of wit or some humorous observation which put all at their ease.

And there was no *pretence*. He really was profoundly interested in what was going on in the wider world and how it affected the lives of those preparing to go out and grapple with its problems. He felt deeply about the relationships between those of different ages, different sexes, different races, different standards of living, different church traditions and he did his utmost to proclaim the way of constructive reconciliation. In doing this he not only pointed to the way of reconciliation in Christ but also became involved in situations of alienation to the point of personal suffering. The way of the Cross was a phrase often on his lips. It was a way which he never shirked in his own ministry, in private prayer and in pastoral compassion.

V

On April 21st. 1963 Joe preached his farewell sermons at Great St. Mary's. There was little reference to the past four years by way of praise or blame, success or failure. Instead his text for the morning sermon was ''I saw a new city'' from which he proceeded to portray his vision of what the future of Cambridge might be though he dismissed any idea of a blueprint or any attempt simply to reform structures. ''Persons come before things'' and the guidelines for personal vocation and personal relationships have been set forth once for all in the career of Jesus himself.

So the preacher painted a picture of Jesus, not fantasising but making out of what is that which should be: identifying himself with the social situation 'completely and absolutely as it is': not being served but in all things serving the community: taking his stand ultimately on a point where he stood alone in loyalty to what he believed to be God's will. What did this all means for the city? ''The city must die in order that the city may live . . . you cannot move without sacrifice. When the new comes, the old must disappear. And that just does not means the bad only must go, it means that the good must go if it stands in the way of the best''.

In the evening the theme was *The Shaking of the Foundations,* a title made famous by a sermon of Paul Tillich's. It was a time when religion had suddenly struck the headlines through the publication of John Robinson's book *Honest to God* and when the moral issue related to the use of nuclear weapons was being dramatised by the protest marches to Aldermaston. Joe was leaving Cambridge at a time when not only ethical and doctrinal foundations were being shaken but the very survival of life on the earth was being called in question. What had Christians to say when stabilities of former years seemed to be collapsing?

Again Joe focussed his hearers' attention on Jesus: "if the foundations of morality do shake, let us rediscover their secret in Jesus". Here was the norm: his attitude to truth, to property, to sex, to life: not condemning publicans and sinners but eating with them, not just defending existing conventions but deepening and extending them. And what was true of morals was true also of doctrine. The foundation is not this or that formula or interpretation or image (the famous newspaper headline had declared 'our image of God must go') but Jesus Christ Himself. "We need the interpretations to throw light on him but if we have sold ourselves to an interpretation instead of putting our trust in him, we are worshipping an idol, and until the idol is smashed, our trust will not be in the foundation that alone is stable".

His final plea was for adoration of God in Christ. He always had a horror of any kind of idolatry — anything fixed, static immovable. His last word might have been that of John, the elder: "Little children keep yourselves from idols". Instead, he recalled what happened on the eighth day after Easter in the upper room and reminded his hearers of the words of Jesus: "Blessed are they that have not seen and yet have come to believe".

Joe crossed the Cambridge sky like a comet, coming out of a very different environment, shining brightly for a relatively short period of four years, and then going out again into a future largely unknown except that it would be very unlike what he had experienced in his time at Great St. Mary's. His sparkling informality in the pulpit would be long remembered as would some of his explosive utterances. But most of all he would be remembered for his intense interest in and concern for *individuals,* his humility, his gentleness, his understanding of the younger generation, his utter devotion to his Lord and Master, revealed in selfless service and imaginative prayer.

10

New Reformation: Ancient Tradition

Rarely can a public appointment have received so delighted and widespread a response as that of Joe to be Bishop of Salisbury. Letters came from all quarters and from all kinds of people. Bishops and clergy, Heads of Colleges and students, ministers of other denominations who had attended his Jerusalem courses, innumerable friends made in Rochester, Truro and Cambridge — all expressed their heartfelt satisfaction that his personal gifts and his devoted service had been recognized by the powers that be.

Yet it is hard to imagine a greater contrast than that between his manner of life and work during his hectically busy four years in Cambridge and that which awaited him in Salisbury. He had come to Great St. Mary's at a time when everthing was on the move and the wind of change was beginning to be felt. In the church itself, Mervyn Stockwood had developed new patterns of corporate worship and fellowship which Joe was altogether eager to maintain. In university circles it was a time of liberation and new permissiveness, a time of questioning and experimenting, and this attitude found its expression in religious circles through the publication of such books as *Soundings, Honest to God,* and *Objections to Christian Belief.* This questioning of traditional standards of faith and conduct gathered such strength that, shortly after Joe's departure, John Robinson coined the phrase *New Reformation.* Whether or not this was justified, the general atmosphere in Cambridge in the early sixties was certainly one of vitality and debate, an eager search for new expressions of the Christian faith which could be related to new developments in society at large.

Joe entered into all this with sympathy and even excitement. Not that he was prepared to align himself with every novel idea or practice. He possessed an active mind, a critical judgement. Yet he was ever ready to fasten on to events happening in the world or to current trends in university life and to submit them to his own radical criterion: How do they stand in relation to the words of Jesus and in particular to his cross and resurrection?

The scores of letters which came to him from members of the congregation of Great St. Mary's after his appointment leave no doubt about the impression he had made during his relatively short ministry there. His sermons might sometimes have been disjointed but they were never dull. They were so obviously spoken out of his own experience that they could not fail to touch deeps in his hearers' own hearts. Even more than the sermons there had been his unceasing interest in and concern for individuals. To establish relationships with *persons* was of paramount importance and herein lay Joe's supreme gift. Five minutes with a couple before their marriage could somehow make an indelible impression on them. He could draw an individual out into a real relationship with himself more quickly, I think, than anyone I have known. And in a teeming university city opportunities for doing this were endless.

I can illustrate this by quoting a few extracts from letters written by members of the congregation when the news was made public in February 1963. "You have thrown everything you have into your work". "Those of us in the town congregation felt how marvellously he drew together the town and gown threads and built up a wonderful sense of fellowship". "What I think makes me most happy is the knowledge that this promotion won't change you at all — you will still, I know, have time and friendship for the humbly placed people whatever class or colour — and that can be said of few". As for his sermons and more informal talks: they "have always spoken directly to my condition and been of immeasurable help". "As I have often told you before, I've never listened to anyone who has preached so destructively/constructively, so consistently denouncing the sham and showing the real and doing it all with what you yourself call 'fun in religion'". "Many times just that odd sentence you have given from the pulpit has helped our youngest boy who is now going through that difficult teen-age time". And a note from a College Chaplain must have warmed Joe's heart: "If you could know how often in an undergraduate discussion someone says, 'But in Joe Fison's sermon last Sunday'".

One of the most charming letters, and perhaps least expected, came from a noted Cambridge 'character', the Rev. F. A. Simpson of Trinity College, who had preached a notable sermon at Mervyn Stockwood's consecration.

"What is so especially satisfactory about this is that it would never have happened if you had stayed comfortably preaching to a few old ladies in Lincoln. But because at the dictate of conscience you came out into a strange land — leaving behind you I imagine many of the amenities of existence — it has been made up to you in this present life: a thing that so seldom visibly happens that it is particularly pleasant to see when it does".

So Joe and Irene left Cambridge with, as one expressed it, 'universal good-will' mixed, as another said, with 'consternation' so far as Great St. Mary's was concerned. A former curate in the Far East 'danced jigs', while a former member of the congregation was said to have 'let out uninhibited whoops for joy'. But there were also messages of 'commiseration'. All were agreed that the Cathedral Close at Salisbury was a place of exquisite beauty and that the diocese was one of the 'nicest' in England. But was it not also one of the most conservative? Could Joe make the leap from the youthful enthusiasms, the ferment of new ideas, the sense of a new reformation, the deepening of spiritual life such as he had known in Cambridge to the ancient traditions, the often formal church-going, the rural communities, the dominantly agricultural economy such as he would find in Wiltshire and Dorset?

One letter began: "Poor old Joe! If ever a chap needed praying for it's you". It came from an incumbent in the Salisbury diocese and continued: "coming with your fire and zeal and love into a situation where the sheer weight of the machinery of the 'Establishment' will do its best to squeeze the spiritual life right out of you. God help you to bear up under the incubus till you can consign it to where it belongs!". Another incumbent wrote: "Whilst nothing can give me greater joy than a closer proximity to you and yours, I find I can understand from Great St. Mary's congregation to Southwark but not to Salisbury with its 600 parishes of scattered population and aging and retired clergy". And in more general terms the distinguished liturgical scholar, Professor E. C. Ratcliff wrote: "What a loss to Cambridge! But then you possess all the qualities of a *Pastor bonus* and it is right that you should exercise them as a Bishop. I do hope that you will cut through Committees and reorganisations and Five year Plans and Purple Tape of every kind, and give the English Episcopate a new 'image'. But you are sure to do so. It's no matter for congratulation nowadays to become a Bishop: so, instead, I send all best wishes and promise prayers". This wish for a 'new image', or perhaps a rediscovered image, was echoed by Principal Whitehorn of Westminster College: "As an admirer of old Richard Baxter, I adhere to his liking for 'primitive episcopacy' as opposed to 'prelacy and the diocesan frame': and I think that you will be happier that way also. So I hope and pray that the blessing of your ministry as 'pastor pastorum' will not be burdened by administration beyond compatibility with 'ministry'''.

There was certainly no likelihood of Joe becoming a 'prelate'. As an old friend put it: "It will be so good for the church to have another human being on the episcopate". Moreover there were precedents for not being overwhelmed by administration. Dr. G. A. Chase, formerly bishop of Ripon, who had retired to Cambridge wrote: "I remember that most of the letters I received when my announcement was published were consolatory! They seemed to think I was in for a miserable existence consisting of problems and committee work. Don't you believe it. Of course there are problems and there is committee work. But most of my time was spent pastorally — visiting and helping the clergy (most repaying), confirmation etc (most refreshing), and even 'do's' after parish events (a grand chance to meet the laity) . . . I do want you to have at least one cheerful letter, 'congratulating' you on the chance of a grand job".

Perhaps the biggest surprise to many was that Joe should have been appointed to *Salisbury.* Some thought of him as eminently qualified for the bishopric in Jerusalem when next it fell vacant. Others could imagine him in a see containing civic and university life. But as chief pastor in a diocese whose first bishop was appointed in 1075 and in which Joe would be 74th in succession: a diocese moreover in which nearly 80 years had passed since a man was appointed its overseer (as Joe put it) straight 'from the ranks', his immediate predecessors having been translated from other English dioceses or in the case of St. Clair Donaldson from an Archbishopric overseas: this seemed to make it all the harder to imagine how a man famed for his thunderous exclamation 'Down with bishops!' could ever fulfil an episcopal vocation in ways expected of him.

Yet his decision was made. Undoubtedly he had been feeling the strain of the dual responsibility at Great St. Mary's. It did not help that the Vicarage was 2 miles away from the Church and that at first there were quite inadequate facilities for study or interviews in the Church itself. The task of arranging for visiting speakers and preachers months ahead is exceedingly arduous and in term time there is scarcely any chance to relax. Joe managed to lead a pilgrimage to Greece and Palestine while still at St. Mary's but it is questionable how long he could have sustained the constant pressures of the Cambridge task.

Moreover, there had been a subtle change in the make-up of undergraduates coming up to Cambridge after Joe's first two years at Great St. Mary's. Until then the majority came as older men, having first done a period of national service. But most of the new arivals in 1960 came straight from school and with these Joe found it much harder to come to terms. I think it was true of him generally that he was never quite at ease with adolescents. He was happy with children and entirely at home with those who were beginning their careers in church or state. But adolescents looked at him more cautiously and did not always respond to his complete open-ness, his witticisms and his attempts to establish positive relationships immediately. At any rate the second half of his time at Great St. Mary's seemed harder as far as undergraduates were concerned and, as he was nearing 57, he may well have felt that it was time to move on. But if he was to move, to what position would it be if not to a bishopric? The opportunities such a post presented for leadership and pastoral care appealed to him. So too did the varied character of a bishop's life. Cambridge had been a grand experience but now he had the conviction that the call to Salisbury was one which he could not refuse.

Perhaps the shortest news-item concerning his appointment appeared in the *Daily Scandal,* the official newspaper of his son David's preparatory school. It read: "Fison's father has become head of Salisbury Cathedral, the highest spire in England".

III

The consecration took place on St. Mark's Day (happily, for Joe had a special love for St. Mark's Gospel), April 25, in Southwark Cathedral. He was presented to the Archbishop of Canterbury, Dr. A. M. Ramsey, by the Bishop of Ely, Dr. N. B. Hudson and the retired Bishop of Truro Dr. E. R. Morgan. Some thirty bishops assisted in the consecration and the present writer was privileged to preach the sermon. Large numbers of friends travelled from Truro, Cambridge and other parts for a truly joyful occasion. After a brief holiday-retreat Joe took full charge of his new office when on May 24th, he was enthroned in the Cathedral Church of the Blessed Virgin Mary at Salisbury (referred to by one of the Canons of Winchester as that 'majestic and elegant Cathedral').

The splendid ceremony included some ancient features peculiar to Salisbury. The Bishop first robed in Mitre House, (then a dress shop). Inside the Close the Diocesan and Cathedral dignitaries, the Mayor and Corporation, and the Choir formed themselves into a square while a boy, chosen to be the Bishop's Chorister, addressed the Bishop in a somewhat lengthy Latin speech. Aftr the Bishop had made his reply (also in Latin) which he saw fit to intone because he had learned that the Bishop of Salisbury is the official Precentor of the Southern Province, all moved on to the Cathedral.

It was a beautiful day and the traditional ritual for the 'Induction, Enthronement and Installation' of a Bishop was duly performed. But by general consent the most memorable event was the Bishop's sermon, surely unlike any other preached on such an occasion, either in Salisbury or elsewhere. It was characteristic of Joe that a word, a phrase, an idea, a story, would suddenly capture his attention and imagination and then he would weave around it material appropriate for particular occasions or settings. Some times before leaving Cambridge he was seized by the thought that Jesus at his baptism stood in one of the lowest places on earth, if not altogether the lowest — the place where the Jordan flows into the Dead Sea. In such a place, he could not do other than look *up:* up to his Father, up to his fellow-men. And in such a place, Joe concluded, every true Christian ought to take up his own position. Therefore on his enthronement day he conceived himself not, as the schoolboy paper put it, as the 'head of the highest spire in England' but as following his Lord in descending (Ephesians 2. 9.) first to the lowest level. "My enthronement to-day will be a farce and indeed almost a blasphemy unless it has behind it some remotely similar background. All eyes then on the descent. We can leave the ascent to God".

The sermon was completely original, utterly sincere. I doubt whether any other that he ever preached expressed more movingly and more comprehensively the Gospel which he tried to proclaim, the ideal of ministry which he tried to embody, and the attitude to others of whatever creed or class or nationality which he tried always to maintain. It was brilliantly worked out with vivid pictures of Jesus — "He looked up to Mary his mother though that didn't prevent him from breaking her heart. But he also looked up to Mary Magdalene and that enabled him to save her soul. He who saw through all pretenses and shams and who knew the worst that was in man, nevertheless chose to look up to all men. That was how in him and through him God so loved the world that he saved it". He spoke too of John Wesley, whose heart was strangely warmed on May 24, 1738, only after days in which he had been in the depths, near to despair: and of the publican who out of the deep cried 'God be merciful to me a sinner'. After appealing to the piercing words of Jesus: "The princes of the Gentiles exercise dominion . . . it shall not be so among you". "The Son of Man came not to be ministered unto, but to minister" he declared.

"The slavery most of us would give anything to get out of, Jesus chose to get into".

The words and example of Jesus and his true followers provided the framework of the sermon. Filling it in came some of Joe's characteristic illustrations, drawn from well-nigh every aspect of contemporary life — international, social, political, industrial, religious — to drive home his message that what Jesus had done in descending first was what needed to be done in every department of life if the world was to be saved. "Let's come nearer home — think of the transformation in national and civil politics, if Conservatives looked up to Socialists and if Liberals looked up to both — and vice versa too!". "In every town and village of this Diocese, the Church should look up to the Chapel and the Chapel should look up to the Church". "What about the relations between Wiltshire and Dorset, the Cathedral and the Diocese, between so-called 'dignitaries' and the so-called 'inferior clergy'? Are we looking up to one another or prhaps trying not to look at one another at all?". He ranged over the divisions in the world, in society, in the Church and then, again characteristically, pointed the finger straight at himself.

"I as your Bishop must set you an example. That isn't going to be at all easy. In fact it's going to be quite impossible unless I'm very low down. For it isn't any good my pretending to look up to someone I really despise. Laurens van der Post is right: its the look in the eye that matters; either it's genuine or it's worse than useless. And it can never be a genuine upward look unless I'm lower down than the person I'm looking up to. Of course that's where I really am. I don't have to go down to the Dead Sea. I only need to remember that I'm in the presence of the living God. If I stay there, it won't be long before I get glimpses — perhaps through the words of others — of my ignorance and weakness and sin. But it's so easy to forget God's presence and then to imagine that I'm not so low down after all, but really quite high up.

"Surely, if we try to answer these questions honestly, we are all brought to our knees, down where we should be, to the place from which God can lift us up. But that's all we need: to adopt afresh the posture to which, as the brotherhood of the baptized, our baptism has committed us. If we would do that, then baptismal regeneration would come alive in our own experience and we should find we were being continually born again. Our religion wouldn't cease to be deadly serious, but it would also become tremendous fun".

After applying his central insight to the family and to the

work of the missionary he concluded by a contrast which caught the eye of the press. Pointing out that 'looking up' didn't imply an indiscriminating blurring of the distinction between beauty and ugliness, between right and wrong, he declared: "St. Paul could blast as well as bless — and so could Jesus . . . We can blast off bombs to-day but we seem to have lost the power to blast in Jesus' way . . . The blast-off must have behind it the upward look — and so must the blessing". His final words set the tone for his nine years as Bishop of Salisbury.

"My past has been catching up with me these last three months. How often I used to say 'Down with all Bishops'. And how often recently I've been made to eat my own words! Perhaps to-day's call to me isn't to repent of the phrase (not, at any rate in so far as it now applies to me), or to scrap it, but to face up to it and redeem it. If I were truly to come *down* and serve you, then — and only then — I should look up to you. I can't rightly be a bishop, an *episcopos,* and oversee or look-over you (which is what the Greek word means) unless I look up to you. Without this upward look episcopal blessings as well as episcopal blastings may do far more harm than good.

"Our Lord's public ministry on earth ended with his ascent from the Mount of Olives. It began with his descent to the River Jordan. The two places are twenty or thirty miles apart, but they're in full view of one another — the highest and the lowest places in the vicinity. How our earthly ministries will end, we must leave with God. How they begin, or begin afresh, is our responsibility. Aren't we all called to 'begin with shame to take the lowest place' (Luke 14. 9. N.E.B.)? Not in body, for we can't be at the Dead Sea; but in spirit, for we are in the presence of the living God. From any other position the upward look is so often only a hollow sham.

'Two went to pray? O rather say
One went to brag, th' other to pray
One nearer to God's Altar trod
The other to the Altar's God'.

That is Richard Crashaw's poetic paraphrase of Jesus' parable of the Pharisee and the Publican. Spoken about the Jerusalem Temple long ago, it applies to Salisbury Cathedral on May 24th. 1963. 'That he ascended, what is it but that he descended first . . .'. 'Out of the deep have I cried unto Thee, O Lord: hear my voice'. The opening of the heavens and the warming of the heart we must leave to God: the cry from the depths must come from ourselves".

After the excitement of the Consecration and the Enthronement, Joe and Irene set to work to make South Canonry a comfortable home, a centre for hospitality and a convenient base for the bishop's manifold activities. It is a lovely house, not too large, with ample garden (which Irene loved) stretching towards the River Avon which runs past its boundary. It stands on the edge of the Close, regarded by many as the most beautiful in England.

After the struggles with housing problems at Rochester, Lincoln and Cambridge it seemed that now at last the family could settle into an ideal home in idyllic surroundings. But this hope was badly bruised when, less than a year after they had moved in. Joe returned to Cambridge to preach at Great St. Mary's and was shattered by a telephone call telling him that his house was on fire! Hugh Montefiore, his successor at the Church, has described the incident vividly:

"He had lunch and retired to his bedroom, saying that nothing on any account should disturb him as he had to work on his sermon for that evening. Five minutes later the telephone rang.

"I must speak to Bishop Fison"

"I'm very sorry you can't, he has said he won't be disturbed"

"I must speak to Bishop Fison"

"I told you you can't"

"Tell him his house is on fire".

"And when I did tell him all Joe would do was to stand looking out of the window saying 'Oh dear, Oh dear, Oh dear' — and then he preached a simply marvellous sermon on 'Evil' that evening". (It's title was: What it means to me 'to renounce the devil'). Joe did not miss the opportunity to suggest that the devil might already have been busy on that day.

Irene had returned to Salisbury immediately and found, to her relief, that the structural damage was not very extensive. An office had been burnt out completely, with the serious loss of Joe's official diary — the only record of his future engagements. Thick black smoke had reached every room upstairs except the guest-room suite so that walls, curtains, ceilings and the contents of every drawer and wardrobe were coal black. Joe and Irene were full of praise for the prompt and efficient work of the Salisbury firemen and entertained them later in their home. It was a temporary setback but the fire did not reach Joe's lovely study, a haven in which he could snatch brief periods for preparation of his innumerable public utterances, a quiet setting for the countless personal interviews to which he gave himself so generously.

From the home he now had to travel out great distances, often returning late at night from parish events. From Marlborough and Andover down to Wimborne and Poole and westwards to Dorchester, Weymouth and Lyme Regis the diocese extends, embracing the counties of Dorset, most of Wiltshire, and even some parishes in Hampshire. Salisbury, though well situated for Wiltshire and East Dorset, was far removed from the western half of that county, and many proposals had therefore been made for making Dorset a separate diocese. But as has been found in other parts of England, tradition and finance operate together to hinder partition.

Joe had the loyal and devoted assistance of Victor Pike, Bishop of Sherborne, but the very structure of the Church of England makes it impossible for the suffragan to relieve the diocesan of many of the most burdensome of his duties. If Joe's reponsibilities could have been confined to Wiltshire, the strain would have been less and he might have been able to make a more valuable contribution of the Church at large.

However, although he never had the assistance of a second Suffragan, the Church Commissioners allowed him a full-time Lay Assistant and full-time Lady Secretary. Together these dealt with the more official sections of the Bishop's diary and voluminous correspondence though he was indefatigable in writing short and often witty letters in his own hand. The Diary was planned to cover 3 years ahead, with the immediate future divided into 15 or 30 minute sections allowing estimated times for meetings, journeys, interviews etc. Full scope was allowed for the generous hospitality which he and Irene planned for the monthly Staff Meeting, for the Conference of Rural Deans, for the Cathedral Chapter, for the summer party for clergy and wives and for the Diocesan staff in Church House, More casual visitors were also sure of a welcome: Joe seemed not to forget anyone and always made himself available for all the time that was necessary to anyone with serious problems, even if it left him with no free time at all.

He did occasionally relax and go off for a brief holiday. One such contained an episode which his family has not forgotten. He and Irene went one day to Abbotsbury where they completely relaxed. Joe's holiday wear was very old clothes with an ancient tie replacing his clerical collar. Towards the end of the week they came across a local pottery where Irene bought two flower-vases, probably taking quite a time in choosing them. Then they passed the village shop and she remembered that she needed stamps for post cards. Joe didn't enjoy shopping and rather grumpily said he would stay outside, hoping that she wouldn't be long. However there was quite a delay for the one lady serving was busy with customers at the grocery counter while Irene waited for her stamps. At length she emerged expecting that by this time Joe would be not a little cross at having had to wait so long. Instead she found him bursting with laughter as he said good-bye to a local man. What had happened was that while standing by the shop door in his scruffy clothes, looking very glum and holding the two pots in his hands, the passer-by took pity on him and put a penny into one of the pots!

V

Before I record some of the events of his Salisbury career, I want to summarize a very interesting paper which Joe wrote about the Christian ministry in general with special reference to the Episcopate. It helps us to see how he conceived his own calling and how he tried to organise his own work.

The Diaconate, he wrote, can only with difficulty be regarded as a separate order for the whole church is called to *serve* after the pattern set forth by Jesus himself. Deacons may be set apart to perform special functions but only as representatives of the Church at large. Presbyters are eldermen or aldermen, bearing special responsibilities by virtue of their seniority in learning or experience. The bishop does not cease to be a servant or an elder but in addition is an overseer and a visitior. In Jesus "past, present and future combine, and in the Christian minstry they must also combine. And how? Would it be fanciful to suggest that the Diaconate represents him who is serving the present; the presbyterate represents him who was preserving that past; and the episcopate represents him who is to come, pioneering the future?".

He went on to expand his conception of the bishop's role:

"The bishop is pre-eminently the pastor, the shepherd. But the shepherding suggested by the pattern of the Good Shepherd is not that primarily of keeping the flock together, but rather of leading them forward — and by so doing, and only by so doing, keeping them together. Within the church, as well as outside it, anarchy is due not ultimately to a breakdown of law but to an absence of vision. The law obtains credibility if it serves and is seen to serve a worth-while and desirable goal. It is a means, not an end; at best a schoolmaster to bring us to Christ. As a means, it is essential; as an end, it becomes intolerable. It was in an era of their history when it was in danger of becoming quite intolerable that the writer of Proverbs gave to his people the great word: ''Where there is no vision'' (perhaps it could be translated, 'prophecy') ''the people perish'' (and certainly it should be translated, 'cast off restraint') (Proverbs 29:18)

''A bishop must be a father — that is the clear implication of the seniority of the *presbuteros*. He must maintain the past tradition of the elders. That is at least part of his apostolic succession. But he will know that tradition can only be maintained, against those who would break it downwards, by those who are willing to break it upwards. Therefore he will not stifle the initiative of his spiritual children: he will encourage it. But will he — when it comes to the crunch? Or will he fall back on the exercise of an authority after the ultimate pattern, if not of the Grand Inquisitor, certainly of the Victorian parent? Or will he abandon all authority and abdicate, after the manner of so many modern parents? He will not be able to speak with authority, if he does not know the authorities, but merely knowing the authorities will not enable him to speak with authority. He will only do this if he is himself ''a man under authority''. ''I also am a man set under authority''. (Luke. 7:8) Am I?

''But a bishop must also be a bishop. There must be something truly apostolic about him in a sense that that word does not apply to the whole church and to deacons and presbyters. What is this something? Undoubtedly in his liturgical function as chief celebrant of the Eucharist, he stands for the unity of all Christians within the diocese. In his membership of the college of bishops he stands for the unity of all Christians everywhere. But in his literally apostolic calling — in the sense of 'sent out' — he should also stand pre-eminently for the missionary work of the Church. And to him should specially apply the words of the then Governor of Kenya during the Mau-Mau troubles: 'If you cease to want to go out, you had better get out'.

''But perhaps even more important today, the bishop is called to the task of courageous thoughts and action, and I ask for your prayers that we may not totally fail to respond to the call. He must teach. There have been times — and I think this is still true in Greece — when he is the only authorised preacher in church. And he must be prepared to take a lead — not everywhere, but where he is called upon to do so. The Protestant Bishop of Hanover, Hans Lilje, calls especially for this lead, and ends his appeal with these words — 'In the 16th. Century one of the bravest Reformers tried to rouse his bewildered community. Zwingli had this to say to his beleaguered people: For God's sake, do something courageous. That is not bad advice for any bishop who wants to live up to his ecumenical obligations today'. On which I can only comment in the words of Deborah: For that the leaders took the lead in Israel, bless ye the Lord''. (Jdgs. 5:2.)

Perhaps the point of greatest interest in this sketch of the three-fold ministry is that only one reference is made to *sacramental* (no reference to ordination and confirmation) functions. Within the nearly 2000 years of the history of the Church's ministry two dominant strands have been interwoven — the Hebraic and the Hellenistic, the prophetic and the sacramental, the Protestant and the Catholic. And these two strands have corresponded very closely to social and economic conditions: the first to the more mobile, commercial, mercantile, social groupings, the second to the more settled, agrarian, land-based communities. In Joe's delineation of the ministry there can be little doubt that the greater emphasis lay on the first. Yet the diocese of Salisbury was dominantly representative of the second. Could Joe express his ideal effectively in an area whose traditions were amongst its most precious possessions and for which proposed changes often seemed to constitute an unacceptable threat?

11

Deadly serious and tremendous fun

Both in his installation sermon and in his first written message to the Diocese Joe coupled together seriousness and fun. He could doubtless have found plenty of precedents for the former in records of episcopal careers: I wonder whether any bishop had ever before looked ahead to years of 'tremendous fun'. Yet this was no mere bid to attract attention. The future was bound to be full of new adventures, particularly in personal relationships; wherever in his experience there was a real encounter with another human being a spark was kindled and life became exciting.

From beginning to end in his work as a bishop *persons mattered more than things*. In the diocese there were some 300 clergy and these were Joe's first concern. He wanted to get to know them (and soon they were being called by their Christian names) not just in an official way but in the context of their own situations and their own individual needs. There were also ministers of other denominations and soon many of them were happy to regard him as *their* bishop. Yet he would certainly not give disproportionate attention to clergy and ministers. Layfolk, whether or not they were church members, were also his constant concern and because he enjoyed meeting them and talking to them, barriers were quickly swept away.

I have not attempted to collect testimonies from those who remember gratefully how Joe came to them at a time of need or welcomed them into his study or exchanged a cheerful passing word and thereby lightened the day, often by some humourous sally. Instead I have chosen one example which seems to me to typify his pastoral ministry. The note was written by Brother Martin, of the Society of Saint Francis:

"When he first became Bishop of Salisbury he was very keen to meet all the parochial clergy, and he visited Deanery Chapters with this in mind. He came to the Sherborne Deanery Chapter on Corpus Christi day. Being of Evangelical background, from which standpoint he had in some ways moved some distance, he approached the clergy very cautiously, perhaps because in rural Dorset he feared the worst: He began by saying that *some* people were observing the festival of Corpus Christi, adding, "I say 'some people' so that none of the Brothers will be upset" — or some such words. After the service in the Abbey, we met informally for a cup of tea in the Abbey Vicarage. Seeing me in my brown Franciscan habit, the

Bishop said: 'Brother Douglas and I have something in common — we were both curates at St. Aldate's, Oxford. He can't deny it in heaven, and I can't deny it on earth'. (Brother Douglas was founder of the Society of Saint Francis; St. Aldate's is a notable Evangelical church).

"I was myself priest-in-charge of two very small village parishes in the Diocese of Salisbury, namely Hilfield and Hermitage. The Bishop was kind enough to take a great interest in these parishes, and he came and celebrated at the Sung Eucharist three times during his first three years in Salisbury (which incidentally coincided with my last three years there, before I left to work elsewhere). On the first occasion, he was obviously apprehensive as to whether the tradition was wildly Anglo-Catholic, and he said before the service that he must go and inspect the book on the altar. Finding, apparently to his surprise, that it was a large edition of the 1928 Prayer Book, he returned to the back of the church and said quietly, with a large grin (and with apologies to Cranmer) 'It's understanded of the parson'.

"After the Eucharist on all three occasions he met parishioners over coffee in the village hall, and was obviously in no hurry to get away. Then he was entertained by one of the families in the parish. On the first visit he had lunch with Bruce Taylor and family, who lived just outside the village of Hermitage. On the second visit, just over a year later, he asked where Bruce was, since he had missed him. This was extraordinary, since he was obviously meeting scores of people all the time. However, on learning that Bruce was in fact ill, he got his chauffeur to drive him to Taylor's house before leaving, so that he could visit him on his bed of sickness. This quite amazing concern for *people* endeared him to everyone.

"When the appeal for the restoration of Salisbury Cathedral was made, my Father sent a small amount, addressing it to the Bishop (as directed) and mentioned the family connexion. He was delighted and amazed to receive a reply in the form of a letter written by the Bishop in his own hand.

"My own work as a Friar of the Society of Saint Francis took me off elsewhere, and I was five years away from the Diocese of Salisbury when I was later appointed to be Vicar of S. Benet's Church, Cambridge. On the occasion of this appointment I had to write to the Bishop to ask him to cancel my license (which I had kept, with his permission, while I had been away) in order that I could be beneficed in the Diocese of Ely. Whereas this was a legal formality, which would in many cases have been dealt with by a Secretary impersonally, it in fact was greeted with a letter in the Bishop's own hand, wishing me well, assuring me of his prayers, and saying that he hoped that I wouldn't find the central heating system at S. Benet's too noisy! This was absolutely characteristic of him, and showed incidentally that he really did know about the church to which I was being sent.

"I shall always remember him for his great pastoral love, and for his real interest in all those whom he met. When talking to him, one could have gained the impression that his principal interest was in oneself. Naturally this was precisely the way in which he treated everyone, and for this reason he became greatly loved in his Diocese".

This example could be multiplied a hundred times. There were never any significant distinctions. Clergy or laity, white collar or blue collar, military or civilian, town or country — he wanted to be available to all and to bring to all some word of encouragement out of the abundance which he had himself received through the Gospel of Christ.

(After writing the above a letter was sent to me, written by Joe in his own hand, to an incumbent in Bradford who had been offered a living in the Salisbury Diocese by a private patron Miss Culley. It is a further illustration of his pastoral concern set within its theological context).

"I came here from Cambridge. You will come from Bradford. The difference in my case was great. It may be in yours too.

"Therefore the first essential is that you come accepting wholeheartedly and ungrudgingly and with no ulterior motive the church as it is (i) in its geographical situation (very near Swindon and very far indeed from the Diocesan H.Q. at Salisbury (ii) in its peculiar social pattern and way of life (neither utterly rural nor urban — rather hard to make it a centre of life because so much life is focussed for youth on Swindon) (iii) in its churchmanship neither extremely high or low, with a splendid tradition of Stewardship and with (I believe) good ecumenical relations. And, if you are at all like me, you will only begin really to realise what this acceptance means after you have been here for a year or two.

"Are you prepared for this? I think it is the principle of the Incarnation. Think out the practical details of (i) £.S.D. compare them with Bradford. And if our Diocesan scale isn't good, can you accept it? (ii) belonging to a very rural society (iii) many other things?

"Then there is the second principle and that is the principle of the Atonement: on the yonder side of the acceptance of convention will be coming the challenge to strike out with creative ventures, which will be very costly. This will involve you in things of which at present you have no idea. But when they come on the *yonder,* not the *hither* side of acceptance of things as they are, can you face them or will you just settle down?

"If I could talk to you, there is so much I would like to say. But I need some answer to this letter before I write Miss Culley — and I want it to be what you really think and not what you think the Bishop of Salisbury would like to believe that you thought! All that I have said applies deeply also to your wife — I hope you will discuss this with her before replying (discontent domestically with a new setting and environment can be unsettling)

God bless you and guide you".

II

However no diocesan bishop can avoid responsibilities of administration and the Church of England is so organised that it is virtually impossible for a bishop to delegate in any substantial way. His is the final authority and he has a special concern for appointments to parishes and to official positions in Diocese. His problems have multiplied in the course of this century, partly through the increasing mobility of the clergy, partly through the amalgamation of parishes, partly through the diminishing of financial resources. Moreover the diocese of Salisbury was one of the few in England possessing an almost exclusively rural character. It was far from easy to provide a change of scene and manner of work for a man who had perhaps served for a period of ten years in a particular rural parish.

After four years in the Diocese Joe quoted a passage from his speech at the Diocesan Conference in the Diocesan Leaflet:

"I think the present method of clerical appointment and payment is causing great agony and hardship. Hard cases make bad laws. But a Bishop's agony when he cannot find a suitable living for one of his priests within his own Diocese — and this happens all too often in my experience — is only matched by his agony when he is quite unable to remedy a disastrous parochial situation, either because of the undefinable operation of a patronage system which sometimes seems hopelessly out of date and out of touch, or because of the intransigeance of some incumbent who (if he could only see it) has so often turned his freehold into his prison. I do not want to see an increase of episcopal power irresponsibly exercised — I look to Synodical

Government to save us from the inevitable corruption of all power, not least episcopal — and the sooner the better. I do not want the dead hand of a bureaucratic committee to replace the living touch of a Bishop's concern, . . . pastoral oversight and care — I look to Synodical Government to help me here also. I am quite sure some change is badly needed in an understanding of ministerial vocation and it is long overdue''.

Joe did not employ the word 'agony' lightly. He really did agonize over the personal problems of others, sometimes in sympathy, sometimes in 'wrath'. He could never be detached and indifferent. He soon found that his efforts to lead the Diocese forward, to initiate changes, to break through conventional barriers, were far from universally welcomed. There was resentment, there was criticism of a kind which he had not previously encountered. And because he was a deeply sensitive man, these things hurt. They would not deflect him from following what he believed to be the way of Jesus but he became increasingly aware that this was the way of the Cross. Yet paradoxically and marvellously it could still be 'tremendous fun'.

At the end of his first year he wrote a synopsis of the practice of episcopacy as he had experienced it. It had been twelve months of *very hard work*. The daily post took on monstrous proportions so that Sunday became a real holiday. There were letters about confirmation dates, marriage tangles, schools business, and, most of all, about clergy and livings, part requiring only a rubber stamp, part needing reference to other officials in the Diocese. The flood of letters was normally followed by interviews involving deep personal problems: restoration of people to communion, 'living with insolubles and getting the blame', trying to make decisions without any precedent to help.

Then there was committee work. Inside the Diocese, more than a dozen committees or boards; outside, the Church Assembly, the Church's Council of Healing and the Council of Church Training Colleges. Even more important was the performance of the Bishop's liturgical and legal functions — Ordination, Confirmation, Institutions, presiding at eucharistic celebrations — and the preaching of sermons for special occasions. He was constantly going out to parishes, ''(with prayers in the car going out and a chat with the chauffeur coming home). I thoroughly enjoy Confirmations and Institutions (and he never hurried to get away from the inevitable 'bun-fight' that followed). I am just off this week to dedicate the restored spire of the church which was struck by lightning just after I had instituted the new Vicar and it was my first institution after becoming Bishop. It is quite true: anything may happen".

If all this outward activity was to be sustained there had to be personal prayer and Bible study, some acquaintance with works of scholarship, a continuing dialogue with the wider world and at least some recreation. Still he was able "to laugh at himself: otherwise life would be unbearable".

At the end of two years a representative of *The Salisbury Journal* sought an interview and these were some of his questions and answers:

Q. Would you agree that the man in the street regards the Church in many ways as "Parson's Pleasure", and feels quite content to let them get on with it?

A. I think the trouble is he often thinks it is not the parson's pleasure, but the parson's chore! Maybe sometimes he has hit the nail on the head there. But to come to the main point, our greatest need, as I see it, is to organise our whole life and work, worship and witness, so as to start where the mythical 'man in the street' is, however risky this may be — in our words and deeds and in every kind of way. This is the way of the Incarnation, and I think all our work ought to be overhauled with a view to asking the question — is it organised to help people as they are, where they are? Is it trying to meet their real needs, or is it trying to prescribe for what we think ought to be their needs?

Q. What would you look back on as the most outstanding event since your enthronement?

A. At the moment, the most vivid event is the meeting with the churchwarden of a Dorset church who said to me: "We are very conservative in Dorset; we don't want to change", and I loved him with all my heart for saying so. (We got quite a big change a little time after!)

Q. What has been your most shattering disillusion since becoming Bishop?

A. Certainly, about myself, and not about the diocese; an awareness (a) that I cannot push the diocese around and (b) that I ought not to want to, and (c) that only if I take those two facts into my system will anything ever happen that God would like to see happen. And I am quite sure there are lots of things He would like to see happen.

Q. Looking forward now, instead of backward, what do you see as the greatest need for this diocese at the present time?

A. (a) Something I cannot achieve without a great deal of help — radical overhaul of a parochial system with far too many buildings, etc. to maintain, so that we may, as a diocese, be geared for mission and not maintenance. (b) A fresh realisation by church people and others of the unbelievable wonder and the mercy of God. Either the Bishop and the whole diocese is in aid of making this credible in Dorset and Wilts, or else we are a dead loss, and ought to go out of business!

In this interview he laid immense stress on so organising the whole of life and work as to start with people *where they are* and secondly on making the unbelievable wonder and mercy of God credible within the diocese. One of Joe's greatest achievements was to do just this. He had to be chief speaker at all kinds of functions: school prize-giving, the dedication of bells, the annual service of the Red Cross, a festival of flowers, Plough Sunday, a church anniversary, an ecumenical discussion. He was adept at finding some point of contact and winning confidence and attention at the beginning. But he was never content to pat people on the back or give vague exhortations. By one route or another he seldom failed to reach some striking interpretation of the revelation of God in Jesus Christ. He left his hearers with an appeal not to some orthodox statement of belief but to a vivid picture of Jesus, through his acts or his teaching, revealing the 'wonder and mercy of God'.

To give just one example. It was the Stinsford Flower and Hardy Festival. Joe immediately directed attention to one of his favourite images. Life can be regarded as a circle or as a straight line, but alternatively it can be seen as a spiral — returning to the beginning but a little higher up. He then went back in imagination to the last Hardy memorial service in 1940 when at Evensong hymns were sung which had appeared in *Under the Greenwood Tree,* while through the open door came the scent of roses and carnations and the songs of the birds. Not surprisingly, preaching on this occasion, he took as his text: Consider the lilies, consider the ravens, pointing out that consider means 'get to the bottom', get to the meaning behind. This represented Hardy's own endeavour, still appropriate for to-day. But then Joe turned to perhaps the favourite amongst all the extracts which he liked to quote. It was from Kierkegaard and he loved to tell of an occasion when he and Irene and all the children had been invited to the Savoy Hotel in London. When they arrived they found the room filled with flowers. They commented on the beauty of the display, and their hostess replied: 'Oh yes, the head butler does them'. Joe expressed his delight and started to quote: 'The bird on the branch, the lily in the meadow, the stag in the forest' when to his astonishment the butler broke in and finished the quotation in Danish.

But what were the final words? 'Beneath all these sopranos, as it were a sustained bass part, sounds the *De Profundis* of the Sacrificed, God is Love'. The beauty of the flowers is not enough by itself. What can sustain us when nature seems out of control? He and Irene had faced such a crisis a few evenings before when a torrential storm broke on them while they were on their way to fulfil an engagement. Joe did not tell the full story in his sermon though the whole experience must have been one of the most remarkable in the record of episcopal visitations.

They were travelling on a newly-made double-carriage-way road which had inadequate drainage. They could see that a little way ahead the water was already over a foot deep and rising fast. Behind them a car with a trailer attempted to turn and 'jack-knifed' so Joe attempted to cross the central grassed bank to the eastward side of the road, but the soil was still soft and the car stuck in the mud. Leaving Irene in the car, he paddled back a quarter of a mile to a cottage to telephone but learned that roads were impassable for any aid to come that night. Already he was drenched to the skin but after rescuing Irene and the luggage from the car (which was by then full of water up to the seats) he disrobed completely in the kitchen and spent the night sitting up on a hard chair wearing his pyjamas covered by purple cassock and red chimere and his mitre on his head, (for it was very cold). Irene preferred to lie on the stone floor and with a light rug covering her. There was no food in the house, and the electricity had been cut off by the storm. Out of the darkness came the sound of the bleating of sheep and lambs, struggling in their watery surroundings and it was this that Joe fastened on in his sermon. Can we still believe in God, he said, when we are helpless and all the lights seem to have been extinguished and the sheep may be drowning? "There in the bleating in the waters, as I heard the sheep and lambs, I seemed to catch the echo of the Lamb of God Himself, helpless and bleating on Golgotha, 'My God, my God, why hast Thou forsaken me'. And the words of an old hymn came back to mind (slightly changing the metaphor)

'None of the ransomed ever knew

How deep were the floods? the Lord, came through

Ere he found the sheep that was lost.

Consider Him that endured such contradiction against Himself''.

So Joe began amongst the flowers and the memories of Hardy but before long had drawn upon his own experiences to remind his hearers of the darker aspects of human life in face of which only the message of the Cross can bring courage and hope. Kierkegaard's musical metaphor is in fact peculiarly appropriate to describe his own method in preaching. He was never afraid to repeat a story, a quote, a phrase which had made a special appeal to him. It could serve as a recurring theme, comparable to that within a musical composition. He would weave fresh thoughts and experiences around his basic theme, not repeating himself in any wooden fashion but shedding new light on familiar passages by relating them pointedly to contemporary problems and needs.

So he went to and fro on his parochial visiting, sometimes preoccupied with some pressing issue and misjudging the occasion (at a Marlborough College confirmation his sermon was a passionate denunciation of the atomic bomb. As a parent of one of the boys commented: 'It was marvellously inappropriate to the occasion. Did his compassion for the human race at times affect his judgment?'), sometimes hasty in his interventions, sometimes tired and below his best. But there could be no doubt about his zest, his self-giving and his love of people. And through it all he somehow retained his sense of fun.

III

At Rochester and at Truro Joe had been accustomed to dealing with individuals and to travelling hither and thither to preach and conduct quiet days (which were often very noisy!) But to preside at a Diocesan Conference was quite a new experience. He would need to be well-informed on such matters as finance and procedure and would be called upon to chair debates which could often labour inordinately over minor details.

He was determined to make the conferences as personal and as spiritually uplifting as possible and to this end arranged for a more informal place of meeting in the spacious new City Hall (coffee and refreshments would be available in the foyer: "I have run into trouble with this suggestion because it has been suggested that more people will sip coffee than will listen to speeches. To which I reply, Hallelujah. It will put us all on our mettle to see that the speeches are worth hearing") and for a midday eucharist in the Cathedral. His major responsibility, however, was that of giving the presidential address, declaring his own policy and giving a lead to the diocese on important matters. This he gave for the first time on October 16, 1963.

Having paid a graceful tribute to his immediate predecessors in the see and to his colleagues who had carried on in the interregnum he plunged at once into the swirling waters of 'South Bank' religion and the *Honest to God* debate — topics which had so recently captured the headlines. As always, after a few pungent remarks, he directed the hearers' attention to Jesus himself. Was he ever criticized? A gluttonous man and a wine-bibber? He is beside himself? ''To be faced with both accusations, of worldliness and of religious madness, and to be guilty of neither — this would seem to be the hall-mark of the true disciples of our Lord Jesus Christ, who was himself so accused. Can the Body, if it is loyal, hope to escape what happened to the Head?''.

He then turned to one of his favourite themes — the reformation of the Church of England. If Rome could do it (Vatican 11 had just taken place) why could not Canterbury? ''I am deeply concerned that as a Church we should be both loyal to our doctrinal, liturgical and ethical standards, and also free to reformulate our expression of them. I long neither for dead rigidity nor for anarchy: but for creative living''.

Finally he came nearer home to the Salisbury Diocese itself and set out his very deep *concerns.*

First and foremost, our images of God as Father or Shepherd needed to be redeemed to their true significance. Then *principles:* what Hans Kung calls *subsidiarity* and *stewardship.* The first relates to the settling of church problems by appeal to a subsidiary authority and not on every occasion to the final authority. Joe was appealing for attention to be paid to the diocesan 'chain of command' rather than for everyone to seek direct access to himself. The plea has frequently been made but as often it has fallen on deaf ears. No one could have made himself more accessible than Joe did and he could no avoid the consequences.

A far more delicate issue was that of stewardship. It was a time when stewardship campaigns, though often resisted, had made a degree of progress in the Church of England. But Salisbury lagged far behind most other dioceses. More serious was the matter of the Quota. ''I cannot pretend that I enjoyed going to the Church Assembly for the very first time in my life and finding my Diocese the only diocese in the Provinces of Canterbury and York not paying its quota in full to the central funds of the Church''. And the shortfall in 1963 would be greater than in 1962. So Joe took the daring step (and if there is one matter on which the layman thinks he knows better than the clergy it is on that of finance) of launching his own appeal to deal with the immediate situation and to remove what he regarded as the default of the Salisbury Diocese. He realized that a long-term solution was still needed and this could only be found by an attitude to giving which conformed more closely to the Biblical pattern which he proceeded to expound.

Finally from images and principles he moved on to what was for him most important of all — *persons* and especially the parish priests. His ambition was to serve them. This did not prevent him from making some critical observations. Vicarage gardens? Visiting? The manner of taking services? "I am concerned about the way we clergy use our voices in church. The tape-recorder has been invented. We are without excuse if we do not use it!''.

The address concluded with a final plea for greater co-operation in rural deaneries and for a greater readiness on the part of all to live not for themselves but by the spirit and example of Him who laid down his life for the sheep. It was a fine discourse. The press found a verb to headline the Bishop's first presidential address. He had *lashed* the Diocese for its failure to pay up!

No happier example could be found of Joe's humility and generosity of spirit than the section of his address to the Diocesan Conference in 1969 just six years later, when he paid tribute to Colonel Longfield who was retiring from his chairmanship of the Board of Finance.

"Jim Longfield has had to put up with a good deal from me. I am, of course, very ignorant of finance. He is very well aware of that and I do not think he holds it against me. On the principle cobbler stick to your last — a proverb which I find goes back at least as far as Pliny — the Bishop should not meddle in the affairs of the Chairman of the Board of Finance. Looking back I think I meddled. When I came to the Diocese, I found we were the only diocese not paying its quota in full to Church Assembly. This saddened me. I criticized it and I tried my best to alter it. I now think I was wrong. The Diocese did not pay in full because it was not prepared to give the Church Assembly a blank-cheque to raise its demands on the diocese beyond a previously estimated and agreed proportion of our annual income. It was for this principle that Jim Longfield stood out with great courage against the tide of popular Assembly voting. And he has so completely won his point that it is now the accepted policy of the Church Assembly to make triennial budgetary estimates in advance and to revise them every year and to keep expenditure within the agreed estimate of income . . . I am so glad that we are once again paying our quota in full and paying it quarterly in advance. The touchstone of spiritual health is so often to be found in what we give away and I only wish we could give more''.

In Diocesan Conferences subsequent to that of 1963 Joe usually picked up some issue prominent in public affairs or some sentence from a public utterance and gave his own response in the light of the Christian gospel. Then he commented on the major problems confronting the Church — responsibility towards developing churches overseas, ecumenical discussions (and particularly those concerning Anglican-Methodist unity), the Morley report on the future of the ministry. He did all this vigorously and with a freshness of approach which could make well-worn themes interesting. But there was one persisting concern which found expression in one way or another at most of the Conferences. It was the concern for *change,* for looking to the future rather than to some imagined paradisal past. He never wanted change just for its own sake but without continual re-formation there would inevitably be stagnation and ultimately death.

For *theological* support he turned more than once to Hans Kung:

"Anyone who wants the church to die out, to become the grave of God, must want her to remain as she is. Anyone who wants her to live as God's living congregation, must want her to change. Only by changing does she remains what she is. Only by renewal is she preserved''.

And Joe pointed out that this was only another way of saying that what is true of the physical body is true also of the Body of Christ. ''The permanent identity of a living body depends upon its perpetual change''. — a principle which he illustrated by reference to doctrinal and liturgical issues confronting the Church in the 60's.

For more homely support he delighted to tell of a visit to a large farm in the Diocese. After following the tractor-plough in a Land Rover, he finished up by going all over the modern dairy.

"I turned and said to the farmer, 'This looks like Ancient and Modern Revised'. The farmer smiled and, I think, was pleased. The Vicar also smiled and seemed even more pleased. I asked him why. He said 'Well, So and So modernizes his farm or he would go out of business: but he won't let me change a thing in the church: as it was in the beginning . . .!

No change. This was the attitude which he constantly encountered and which he found it so hard to understand. Was it due to a basic fear? It seemed so contrary to the way of Jesus who ''never fought a rear-guard action''. Faith and the future belonged to the very essence of the Christian Gospel and this had never been better stated than by William Temple in his famous mission to Oxford in 1931.

"Faith is something nobler in its own kind than certainty. For us finite beings in this world that which most of all calls forth our noblest capacities into action is always a hazard of some kind, never a certainty. It is when we are ready to stake our lives on something being so, that nobility begins to appear in human nature.

"To adapt our lives with careful caution to fully established certainties is not in the least noble or heroic: it is merely sensible. It is good to be sensible: it is better to be heroic: but it is best of all to be both, although very few of us are. The whole case of religion, through all ages, is that it is a venture, a quest of faith: and it has ennobled men for that reason".

That is the ennoblement, Joe claimed, of which the Diocese stands in need to-day.

IV

Though there was no university in the Diocese there were a number of public schools, a College of Education, a Theological College and, of course, a very large number of church and state schools. Joe was ex officio Chairman of the Governors at Marlborough and was also chairman of the Theological College Council. These offices were his largest responsibilities in the field of education though he welcomed every chance to meet young people as he went about the Diocese.

At Marlborough he had the complete confidence of the Master, John Dancy, for they had been friends before he was appointed Bishop. He gave of his best in time and attention to school business and to special occasions such as prize-giving and confirmation. Nevertheless it was evidently unfair for the Bishop of the Diocese to be automatically saddled with all the matters with which the Chairman of Governors had to make himself acquainted. In Joe's case it became clear that he involved himself deeply and sensitively in policies which had to be discussed and decisions which had to be taken. He could not bring himself to operate as a relatively neutral Chairman and in consequence the Governors finally decided to relieve the bishop of the requirement to be Chairman, while expressing the desire for him to remain a member of the Governing Body.

It must be admitted that Joe was not the ideal chairman of any committee. Professor Owen Chadwick has written this about the Marlborough situation:

"I was a member of the Governing Body of Marlborough

College while Joe was ex officio Chairman. He was no bad chairman. But he was not a good chairman in the conventional sense because if he felt deeply on a point of the agenda he showed it a little too plainly — because he could be seen to begin to agonize — which is not usually a thing that Chairmen are supposed to do. But the business of the meeting worked well, because the hard-boiled governors found him the humble man that he was, and would not dream of sharpening or prolonging the agony which they had to pretend not to see.

''But they did relieve him of the agony when it became possible to do so''.

The second educational institution which demanded his special attention was the Theological College whose buildings were situated in the Cathedral Close. The 60's were a period of serious questioning in the Church of England about the future of theological training. The old system of establishing a number of theological colleges in Cathedral Closes (Ely, Lincoln, Wells, Salisbury etc) was being subjected to severe criticism. The number of ordinands was falling and departments of religion in universities were expanding. Moreover the old idea that learned Canons could contribute lectures on subjects prescribed for examination proved to be less and less true. What future was there for a theological college outside a university context where it could make good use of the facilities there provided?

It was not long after his appointment to Salisbury that Joe had to face this question realistically for the Principal of the College retired. Before trying to appoint a successor a decision had to be made about the wider problem of the College's usefulness and how far it could continue to attract students. On the face of it, the wisest course seemed to be to close the College and perhaps amalgamate it with another. But after going to considerable lengths in seeking advice, Joe somewhat surprisingly decided to go ahead with a new appointment and the choice fell on Harold Wilson, a man who had considerable experience in the field of adult education and a lively interest in the Arts.

He assumed office in 1965 and soon showed that Joe's choice (for he was mainly responsible for the appointment) had been an inspired one. Wilson set to work to make the students familiar with the new methods of communication being used in the modern world and did everything possible to relate the Christian tradition to contemporary life. Numbers increased until the College was overfull; and though this may have been at the expense of other Colleges, it seemed that Joe's decision to keep the College in being had been fully justified. Though unable to devote time to regular lecturing, he maintained cordial relationships with staff and students, backing the Principal in his efforts to make theological education relevant to the life of the modern world.

V

Parishes, schools, colleges — these were the main institutions for which the Bishop felt a major responsibility. The other great insitution in the Diocese was the Cathedral but here the major responsibility lay with the Dean and Chapter. The Bishop had his throne in the Cathedral and acted as visitor but his prerogatives were carefully defined by the Cathedral Statutes and Joe had no desire to infringe them.

An interesting example of his sensitivity in this respect was provided by his practice at meetings of the Greater Chapter which he regularly attended. There is a curious tradition at Salisbury that the Bishop of the Diocese is allotted a Prebendal Stall in the Cathedral (this is unique). This meant that at a meeting of the Greater Chapter, when the Close Chapter occupied the top table with the Dean as Chairman (and at which in former times the Bishop had usually sat) Joe insisted on taking his place with the honorary canons. In the Cathedral and Chapter House the Dean was primus. The Bishop often celebrated and preached but did so as permitted by Statutes or by invitation of the Dean and Chapter.

However, he lived in close proximity to the Cathedral and was in constant contact with its company. He could hardly avoid being involved at least in some measure in two controversies which attracted a great deal of public attention during his episcopate.

The first concerned stained glass. At the beginning of the 19th. century the eight windows of the Chapter House were clear and let in plenty of light but in the middle of the century, when the technique of medieval grisaille was relearnt, the Chapter decided to install stained glass windows which were completed in 1861. During the 1960's, however, the proposal was made by the Canon Precentor, who by ancient statute held responsibility for the glass of the Cathedral, that the Chapter windows, which seemed quite undistinguished, should be removed and this was agreed by the Close Chapter, the Greater Chapter raising no objection.

The process of removal had scarcely begun (Joe suggested to the Dean that it would be wise to store the old glass) when vigorous protests were lodged from the Salisbury Museum, from the County and from the central Cathedrals Commission.

115

It is widely assumed by the public that a Bishop has more authority in a Cathedral than in fact is the case and because of this Joe soon found himself the target for appeals or demands to stop this act of iconoclasm. He did his best to pour oil on troubled waters though he was only minimally responsible for what had taken place. The final outcome was that the removal process was halted and six of the eight original windows remain as they were: the glass of two windows had, in fact, already been destroyed.

The second controversy arose over the decision by the Chapter to accept Barbara Hepworth's *Crucifixion* to be sited in the Cathedral Close. The then Dean, K. W. Haworth, has described what happened:

The Crucifixion, ''came to us, just getting through the High Street gate (it wouldn't have got through either of the other two). This raised feeling and the County Planners intervened again. We had set it on the north side of the cathedral: in the end it went to a less conspicuous site to the southwest. But many people regarded it as most unsuitable against a 13th. century cathedral. The then Chairman of the Board of Finance was particularly vocal and Joe would have had a lot of that''.

Though he had no authority to act in the matter, Joe felt involved, partly because he had been keen to establish links between the diocese and the living stream of contemporary art and with this in mind had in 1967 appointed Professor Moelwyn Merchant to be Chancellor of the Cathedral. Professor Merchant, who occupied the Chair of English in Exeter University, was not only an authority on Shakespeare and Marlowe but was also a sculptor himself and well acquainted with modern painting. Joe greatly valued what he brought to the Diocese, particularly through his lectures at one of the residential Clergy Schools. He knew of his friendship with Barbara Hepworth and that it was through this that *The Crucifixion* had come to Salisbury. It was therefore exceedingly difficult for him to mediate between the protesting parties and the Cathedral authorities.

A compromise was finally reached by a change of site and Dame Barbara greatly appreciated what the Bishop had done to bring this about. Writing to him she said: ''Somehow I feel that good is going to come out of this tribulation. I feel sure that all that you have done to support the Arts of this century will bear fruit just as the Henry Moore bronze is moving more and more people. One has to be patient because although Henry Moore and I thought we had got through the worst forty years ago, the same antagonisms do seem to arise, and one must not flinch in any way at all''.

With all his love for the Scriptures and with all his enthusiasm for the spoken word, Joe had become more and more aware of the influence of *symbolic* forms in the life of religion. In the diocese there were many such legacies from the past — Avebury, Stonehenge, Sherborne Abbey, Wimborne Minster, above all the Cathedral itself. But he was determined to encourage those who were seeking not only to preserve the past but also to adventure into new areas of feeling and to experiment with new forms in the present.

12

Mr. Greatheart

I

One of the finest tributes to Joe appeared in a note written to *The Times* after his death by Mr. Michael Hamilton, the Member of Parliment for Salisbury. It said: "He had too large a heart". And one of the most attractive figures in English literature is Mr. Greatheart who led and cared for the pilgrims in the second part of John Bunyan's story. Nowhere and never, I think, was Joe happier than when he was either leading a pilgrimage or guiding those who had travelled to some area which had special historic associations.

This was supremely the case in his war-years in Palestine. But further opportunities arose when conditions after the war became sufficiently stable for tours to be organised to the Mediterranean and the Holy Land. Joe was often invited to lead such a tour and the response of those under his charge gave ample testimony to his success in this capacity. In April 1964 he was away from Salisbury for more than three weeks as one of the leaders of a party of more than 400 pilgrims, of many denominations, to Athens and Jerusalem with visits to ancillary places of interest such as Rhodes and Venice, Beirut and Damascus. For him it was an opportunity to grasp in a new way the legacy of ancient Greece and Rome to the religious life of the Western world, to recognize the value of cross-fertilisation, and to gain a new vision of what he delighted to speak of as 'the coming great Church'.

In an address shortly afterwards to the Southampton District Synod of the Methodist Church he said:

"I have just come back from an ecumenical pilgrimage. To be received by the Pope and to be told that he had prayed in Salisbury Cathedral 30 years ago: to have shared in a pilgrimage from the scene of the Last Supper down to Gethsamene (where we prayed silently and aloud — Roman Catholics, Anglican, Orthodox and Free Churchmen — and sang "When I survey"): to have been present at a Roman Catholic Mass where (while the Latin service continued at the Altar) a Methodist Minister read the Collect in the vernacular, two Anglican Bishops read the Epistle and Gospel, and a Greek Archbishop read some prayers — to have led bible reading and expositions in English and French with both Roman Catholic and Reformed Protestants taking part in the readings, saying of the Lord's Prayer and the Grace — to have seen the Street of the Knights at Rhodes — witness to a dead heroism, so tragic and so futile (?) — and to have visited the almost embalmed beauty of Mount Athos with its tradition of 1000 years of monasticism, and yet raising in my mind some of the same thoughts as the Street of the Knights — what more can I say? Far beyond me, here were pointers to the Coming Great Church, for which we pray, which more worthily represent the wonder of the glorious Gospel of our Lord and Saviour in the twentieth century''.

However the pilgrimage which probably gave him the greatest thrill of all was that which he led to Ethiopia in the first fortnight of 1971. I give extracts from his report:

''We consisted of three men and nine women: three Roman Catholics two Quakers, one Church of Ireland and six Church of England. We spent six days in Addis Ababa where audiences were arranged with the acting-Patriarch and with the Emperor himself.

''The audience with the acting-Patriarch lasted an hour or more. There was a very friendly spirit. Nearly everyone spoke. And most fittingly, one of our elderly Quaker ladies — who was normally very silent — spoke, as she was led by the Lord, to the acting-Patriarch — a most moving occasion, and a fitting close to an unforgettable afternoon. The audience with the Emperor was arranged at short notice and we talked easily in English. I ventured to close this by reminding his Majesty that, when I had previously met him during his exile, we had closed the interview with silent prayer. I asked him if I might, without impertinence, suggest that we did the same again. He graciously agreed, and we stood for a minute in silence.

''The northern trip by aeroplane was by way of Bahr Dar and Lake Tana to Gondar and Lalibella. Communion on the lake side at Bahr Dar with the sun rising was unforgettable. The lovely lake seemed so like Galilee; only much bigger and of course the water, alas, is not clean, but full of bilharzia, so we had to keep out of it. We spent half a day crossing the lake to go to our Sunday mid-morning service on a peninsula, where the little village with its round church was quite invisible in the trees.

''Off from Gondar to the mediaeval Ethiopian holy city of Lalibella, built as a substitute for Jersalem because the Ethiopians could not make the Palestine pilgrimage in the Middle Ages. Two things stand out in my mind from the Lalibella visit. The first concerns the synchronism of the building of these underground monolithic churches with the building at exactly the same moment of Salisbury Cahtedral. If

119

ever the symbolism of God 'up there' was adequately expressed in architecture, it was at Salisbury, and if ever the symbolism of God, 'the ground of our being', 'down under', was adequately expressed, it was at Lalibella. And the builders had no idea that the two exterprises were going on simultaneously!

"The other memorable event connected with Lalibella was the mule trip high up in the mountains to cliff-face churches along very precipitous ledges and tracks with superb views everywhere and mercifully on the shady side of the mountain. This expedition was inspired by the arrival at Lalibella of some young Irish women teachers from Addis Ababa, who had come over the mountains by mule. Owen Beament seized the opportunity and seven of the party took advantage of it, with Mrs. Barbara King, on a mule, leading right out in front in the Ethiopian colours, a red scarf, a yellow jumper and green slacks!

"From Lalibella we went on to Axum, the ancient holy city of Ethiopia. Lalibella dates from 1200, Axum from 600 or thereabouts. We saw the ancient stelae and the modern church, built by the Emperor. I shall never forget going to the churches at dawn — the chanting and then the processions and the umbrellas and the reading (presumably of the Gospel) in the open air were memorable. But the most moving incident was the spectacle on arrival soon after daybreak of the motionless Ethiopians standing alone *outside* the church praying in a silence that could be felt.

"Perhaps for me, personally, the clearest memory of all was a visit from Addis out to Mulu Farm to see Brigadier and Mrs. Sandford, the oldest British inhabitants of the country, to share their hospitality, to be taken by land-rover cross-country to 'the edge' to see the great precipices down 3000 feet to the valley below, to meet a cousin — to be really in the heart of this ancient Kingdom of Ethiopia in a piece of 'little England': what kindness and what a record of service — *O si sic omnes!*"

But there were also pilgrimages within the Diocese. In June of the same year he was invited to preach to the pilgrims gathered for the Festival at Glastonbury. The words *strangers and pilgrims* from 1 Peter 2:II gave him his cue. Was not the whole point of the Festival to summon us to become once again what we have for so long ceased to be — if we ever were — *pilgrims?* And where in Great Britain better than in Glastonbury to begin again 'to be a pilgrim?' "For if there is one thing that stands out from the mists of Celtic legend, which surrounds our origins here, it is that the Celtic Church travelled light, it hadn't settled down, it was still a pilgrim church, very much on the move".

Joe was fascinated by words and he had become aware that the Greek original of the word synod was used to denote 'fellow-travellers'. Those who travelled with Joseph and Mary up to Jerusalem (Luke 2) constituted a *synodia* (company). So, he suggested, in the year that synodical government was due to begin, the Church of England was being recalled as never before to its pilgrim origins. Yet the first century pilgrims returning from Jerusalem supposed that Jesus was in the company (synod) when in fact he was not — and therein lay the danger. There is more to life than Celtic pilgrimage: there is also Saxon *education,* the next stage in Glastonbury history. Jesus was in the temple asking questions and learning from the teachers: And we can only be in his company if we join him in the process of being educated.

"He wants now, as then, to hear what we have got to say, to ask us questions. He wants us to hear what others have to say and to ask them questions. Again, this is exactly what Synodical Government within our church, as well as Oecumenical Conversations with other churches, and true dialogue with those of other faiths and of no faith at all, invite us to do: give up our one way posture, either of proselytising evangelism (if we are a triumphalist church) or of teaching (if we are clergy) or of listening (if we are laity) and risk the free for all of genuine dialectic or conversation. This is Education, as the Master demonstrated when he was 12 years old. Do not let us imagine that we can improve upon his example. How I wish this monologue in the middle of this service could be turned into a genuine dialogue here and now! Sermons do not need to be scrapped. They need to be redeemed as "the ordered Hallelujah of the congregation', in the words of that great Congregationalist, P. T. Forsyth".

Finally Joe brought his 'fellow-travellers' to the third stage, typified by the shrine itself and the order of St. Benedict — the stage of *holiness,* St. Peter's call to *abstain.* Holiness can go wrong: selfishness can creep in. But then it must be redeemed to its true meaning. He concluded, with a passionate appeal which might have been addressed not only to the pilgrims but also to the Diocese and indeed to the whole Church of England.

"Because others have settled down, there is no reason why we should. Because others have stopped learning and so stopped teaching too, there is no reason why we should. Because others have selfishly tried to save their own souls there is no reason why we should. We can go on: called to be pilgrims, disciples and saints, "let us go on". Two years ago I was on La Verna, where St. Francis received the stigmata. Why should we not in Glastonbury today receive afresh the stigmata of the pilgrim, the disciple, the teacher and the saint?

"Parishioners — you are pilgrims, and pilgrims never settle down."

II

A long extended debate, which was nearing its decisive vote when Joe began his episcopal career, concerned the possible coming together of Anglicans and Methodists within one united Church. There is no doubt about where Joe's *heart* lay. Methodist Chaplains who attended his courses in Jerusalem became devoted to him. When the news of his appointment to Salisbury was made public one of them wrote: "I can't resist saying that you probably know that Methodists are still not quite sure about Bishops! Nothing could do more to help us than to have Bishops like you". In Truro he found himself in one of the historic areas of Methodism and again had the happiest of relations with its members. He supported the open letter advocating intercommunion which was made public during his time at Cambridge. He genuinely 'looked-up' to his Methodist 'fellow-travellers' and rejoiced to be in their company.

But he was well aware of opposition in the Church of England and of the practical difficulties that were involved. He had to preside over debates in his own Diocesan Conference and to share in the proceedings of the Church Assembly when the final vote was taken. He took the matter very seriously and it occupied a dominant place in his thoughts and prayers from the time of his first Diocesan Conference in October 1963 until August 1969 when he set forth his own guidance in answer to the question: Where do we go from here?

The Diocesan Conference in October 1968 was a critical occasion. The Diocese was being asked to give replies to four leading questions about the scheme of Union and Joe did his best to ensure that it should be done with an intelligent grasp of the issues involved. He sought the help of three Proctors to Convocation and of a lay member of the Church Assembly. With scrupulous fairness he presented each man's contribution to the Conference. The first outlined the Unity proposals and declared his support for them. The second, following the lead of Bishop Graham Leonard, was opposed on grounds which could generally be described as Anglo-Catholic; the third was also opposed on grounds which could be called Conservative Evangelical. The layman's view was a mixture, but in general favoured the maintenance of the *status quo*.

Having presented as 'comprehensively and impartially' as he could the varying points of view, he asked the Conference whether it wished him to state his own view at once or to circulate it later. He felt in duty bound to give a 'personal lead' not in order to close discussion but rather to intensify it at the ruri-decanal level.

Being requested to proceed he took up the questions, showing quite clearly where his own convictions lay.. In regard to the proposal for two Stages:

"Cardinal Mercier's words (often quoted by Joe) apply: 'In order to unite you must love (that is Stage II); in order to love you must know; in order to know you must meet one another (that is Stage I). If we venture on Stage I now, we have a firm intention to go on to Stage II but we have no proof that we shall ever achieve it. But that is what it means to walk by faith and not by sight. Stage I is for me a leap of faith. I am prepared to take it".

He had no difficulty with the proposed Ordinal: the crucial question was that dealing with the service of Reconciliation. In considering this, he appealed to three of his own basic principles. The first had been the subject of his enthronement sermon: no looking down, no despising others, no seeking of the highest place. The second was expressed in one of his key-words, Reciprocity. The third he developed at greater length: his reply expresses so vividly his own attitude and approach to spiritual realities that it is worth quoting at length.

"It is said: 'Bishops are laying hands on Methodist ministers and some say this means they are being ordained. Others say that it means nothing of the sort. This is a fatal ambiguity at the heart of the service. I can't take part in it'.

"To this I reply: This ambiguity is nothing new. Not to mention the Bible in which there are many ambiguities (if we take it as a whole), everyone knows that within the Church of England as it is there are those who hold very different views on many things and find support for their views in some part of either the Book of Common Prayer or the Ordinal or the Thirty Nine Articles. I as Bishop live daily with the problem of this ambiguity in this Diocese. Either we are now guilty of hypocrisy in this matter or we are not. We certainly shall be no more guilty of hypocrisy if we take part in the service of reconciliation.

"That is negative, but that is not all. There is something very positive too. Is not the ambiguity a very good thing? Are we not far too fond, in the West, of defining in terms of black and white, either/or, what the East leaves undefined? And by our over-definition have we not sometimes almost killed the nerve of all real religion, the element of mystery and wonder that defies definition? Even our church buildings show this — Salisbury Cathedral — clear cut, cruciform, fixed; St. Sophia in Instanbul — dome on dome and half dome on half dome, no frontiers, time shading off imperceptibly into eternity. We need both. Does not the ambiguity of the Service of Reconciliation get nearer to Lady Julian's words about the Holy Communion than any clearer definition? 'Oftentimes I desired to learn our Lord's meaning in this thing. And fifteen years after and more, I was moved in ghostly understanding and he said unto me,

Wouldst thou learn thy Lord's meaning in this thing?

Learn it well.

Love was His meaning.

Who showed it thee? Love.

What showed He thee? Love.

Wherefore showed it He? For love.

Then understood I that love was our Lord's meaning'.

"What is wrong with asking God to give us what he sees we need without dictating to him in advance what we need? I am personally glad that there is an element of reverent agnosticism about this service. How greatly I wish there were among us a similar reverent agnosticism about so many of the deepest things of our religion, about which we are apt to be dogmatic! For example, can we really improve upon the definition of the Holy Communion attributed to Queen Elizabeth I with all our definitions about transubstantiation, consubstantiation, receptionism, or whatever it may be?

'Twas God the Word that spake it,

He took the bread and brake it,

And what the Word did make it

That I believe, and take it'.

"All definitions of love (even earthly) must be provisional and partial. There is always at least as great a danger of idolatry (through over-definition) as there is of apostasy (through no definition)".

When the proposals for union had been rejected the Bishops were faced with the problem of what to do next. Joe sent out a directive to his clergy, allowing as much freedom as possible in furture relations with Methodists but not permitting concelebration in the strict sense of the term. Clearly he was deeply disappointed but as always looked to the future. Let the Anglicans whenever possible join with Methodists in worship and witness 'endeavouring to keep the unity of the Spirit in the bond of peace'.

In Bunyan's story Mr. Greatheart was by no means exempt
from trials along the way. There were giants to fight and dark
valleys to go through. Joe, too, had his problems. His
infomality and humorous abides were sometimes seen as
flippancy or lack of dignity. His attempts to break through
lifeless traditions and protective shells were resented by those
unwilling to face unwelcome changes. At times his heart may
have run away with him and a more conventional course might
have been the way of wisdom. But he could never be content
with just going through the motions or with meekly following
the custom. He must try to get to the depths of any situation.
Paul Tillich's claim that if you are concerned about *depth* you
are thereby truly religious was often illustrated in and through
some experience of his own.

One of these occurred in connection with the Hardy Festival
in 1968. There was to be an Inaugural Service in Fordington
St. George Church, Dorchester, with which Thomas Hardy
had close associations. Joe accepted the invitation to be the
preacher. The consequence was that for weeks he was in a state
of troubled perplexity, agonising about how he was to fulfil his
assignment.

Hardy belonged so intimately to Wessex and yet Joe had to
admit that he knew little about his career or his writings. He
began to hunt for books and discovered that a man who had
once been at school with him, William Rutland, had written
two books about Hardy. Joe wrote to him, appealing for his
assistance.

"I really am very ignorant of Hardy, as of other vast tracts of
learning — I am more and more conscious of this.

"And I suddenly thought of you. Perhaps you could give me
a clue. I don't want to pretend that Hardy was an orthodox
Christian. On the other hand I don't want to debunk him but
praise him *honestly* in a Christian context. Can I do it? If so
how? Can you give me any help?".

Rutland was then living in Switzerland but the letter reached
him and he replied, referring Joe to important passages in one
of his books and promising to send a synopsis of a possible
sermon. However, Joe also ran across a book by Lois Deacon
which gave an intriguing clue about Hardy's early life.
Gradually he felt that he had discovered something which
would enable him to celebrate Hardy within the context of that
Gospel of which he himself was a steward and a minister.

The particular context on this occasion he decided would be
the Christian understanding of *Atonement*. He discovered that

another great writer, associated in the end with Dorset, had visited Hardy on occasion.

"In Hardy's latter years another lonely man, after agonies of mind, ended his shorter life the other side of Egdon Heath. And these men knew each other. They met each other. And it was the astonishing testimony of the other in a letter written to Robert Graves on September 23, 1923 that riveted my attention:

'There is an unbelievable dignity and ripeness about Hardy. . . He feels interest in every-one and veneration for no-one. Max Gate is a place apart. . . The peace which passeth understanding — but it is felt and is nearly unbearable'.

"The man who wrote those words was Lawrence of Arabia. How could he have found — in all his agony of remorse — the peace which passeth understanding at Max Gate? I can only think of one explanation. T. E. and T. H. each had a dominant urge to do what they did. And in this they were kindred spirits. How can this urge be defined?".

To use one pregnant phrase, it was he claimed, *to make atonement.* Joe proceeded to give a remarkable example of the way the word 'atonement' had been used in a recent newspaper article about Lawrence. He then went on to suggest that it was this same deep urge which motivated much of Hardy's own creative work — to make atonement for the guilt which he felt concerning his early relations with Tryphena Sparks.

"Hardy on this view sought to immortalize Tryphena in literature, having lost her in life. Through his writing comes again and again the note, not just of deep regret, but also of bitter remorse. He longed to right the wrong. We cannot help asking: was his great literary effort at bottom one vast act of atonement? And was it Tryphena's death, even more than the hostility of the critics of *Jude the Obscure,* that eventually caused the flow of novels to dry up, so that the deeps could issue in *The Dynasts* and the Poems?' Was it not strange that Tryphena, before eventually consenting to marry Charles Gale, required him to give her an assurance that he accepted the doctrine of the Atonement?"

Joe then went on to compare Lawrence with Hardy, claiming that each man spoke to the 'deeps' in human nature: "each has a message for those for whom shallow, cheap, proverbial religious and moral platitudes are almost blasphemy and carry no conviction". In a very moving way he pointed to the record of the last minutes of Hardy's life when he reverted to a sorrow of the past, and died with 'a look of radiant triumph' on his face. Had something happened to transcend his earlier protests and outcries against Providence?

"As a protest against a cheap view of the cost of righting wrong, he was heroic. As an object lesson of the futility of the expensive view of the cost of righting wrong he was tragic. As one who at the very end perhaps came to terms with the ultimate truth that what is not cheap *or* expensive is free at great cost to Another, he was 'radiant'. I cannot prove for certain that this is true of Hardy. But this is the truth of the Christian doctrine of the Atonement. Not in forgetting or endeavour or aloofness or submission but

'In acceptance lieth peace'.

"It is entirely beyond our understanding, of course! Otherwise we should never call 'from the deep' and only when 'deep calls to deep' can we hear any answer to our call. And when we hear it, we must accept it. That is all we can do. 'Thy judgements are a great deep' is the third great word of the Psalmist. And on Calvary we plumb the depths of that great deep. *There* is atonement, not on the cheap (which is damnable — as Hardy saw): not at great expense (which is torture — as Hardy and Lawrence knew): but as something completely free at great cost to Another''. Joe concluded by quoting once again and commenting on his favourite extract from the writings of Kierkegaard which ended in *De Profundis.*

It was, I think, one of the greatest sermons that Joe ever preached. He agonised over its preparation, consulting experts, tracking down books, wondering whether his conclusions squared with the evidence. He might so easily have talked about Hardy's celebration of the Dorset country-side or about the literary excellencies of his novels and poems. Instead he strove to set him within the context of the Christian Gospel. He was prepared to stick his neck out — and paid the price for so doing. Probably no sermon that he preached brought him such a volume of protests. In the congregation were some who wanted only to hear praise and they felt that the name and memory of Hardy had been besmirched by the references to his early liaison with Tryphena. Joe did not take these protests lightly. Had he been guilty of causing hurt by his speculations? He experienced something of what St. Paul described as filling up that which is lacking in the sufferings of Christ by his determination to set everything within the context of the authentic Christain Gospel.

IV

Mr Greatheart had to keep company with his pilgrim band through the valley of the Shadow of Death where "a great mist and darkness fell upon them so that they could not see''. After eight years in office, during which he never for a moment spared himself and perhaps never took enough recreation, he suffered a minor collapse. When celebrating one morning he had to sit down and then fainted. He found that he could not concentrate and felt unable to face the strain of certain important services. In consequence his doctors ordered a complete rest.

ailment and it was therefore decided that a period away from the Diocese, under physical and psychological observation, might be beneficial. However no phsical symptoms were discovered and the isolation for psychiatric treatment proved to be a most unhappy experience for Joe which yielded no helpful results. He said afterwards that although he was profoundly thankful that the ordeal was over, nevertheless he was grateful to have learned what it meant to be ''despised and rejected of men''.

He was still convinced that there was some physical cause for his weakness but all the tests and examinations had shaken his confidence. Officially it was stated that he had experienced 'a nervous breakdown' but what did that imply? Suggestions were made about the possibility of early retirement (he was then 64) or of appointment to a less exacting position but neither of these would be even consider. He loved his work in spite of the strain. He dreaded retirement and hoped, after a period of rest, to resume a normal life.

Fortunately a country cottage which he and Irene had recently acquired was available and they went to stay there for the time being. Yet the peace and beauty of the surroundings did little to raise his spirits. In a letter to an old friend he wrote:

''After I left hospital I had a fiendish headache followed by a feeling of utter depression and complete hopelessness, such as I've never known before. . . Biblically all I could think of was the text in the parable of the Prodigal: 'When he came to himself': I think that hit me hard. But things have at last started to look up and I hope the experience, which has been very chastening, will prove salutary''.

Relief had come through drugs prescribed by a doctor friend and in the autumn he was able to return to Salisbury. If only the physical condition could have been diagnosed everyone would have understood and sympathised. As it was, he resumed work with an intensity which was really far beyond his strength. He hoped to continue for a few years more in the job which he loved — though as Irene knew he had a presentiment that it might not be for long. He began to say, apparently lightheartedly 'If I live till then': his family knew that his life on earth might end at any time.

There were problems in the Diocese, some following on the rejection of the proposals for Anglican-Methodist Union. But there was also a problem of a more personal kind in that he must soon face a situation of a character which he had for years advocated in theory but now had to come to terms with in his own family: his elder daugther, a nurse, became engaged to a young and distinguished American Jewish doctor. A straightforward marriage service according to the rites of the Church of England would be impossible.

However it was arranged that after a civil marriage there would be a service of blessing in the Cathedral and this took place on a lovely summer day, June 10, 1972. The trinitarian formula was omitted from the Anglican form of marriage and Joe selected and included some beautiful prayers from the Jewish rite. He conducted the service with that warmth and gentleness and intense personal feeling which were so characteristic of him and, in spite of the physical emotional strain, succeeded in going through both the service and the reception truimphantly.

The bridegroom's parents came over for the wedding and stayed at South Canonry. Joe won their hearts almost at once. The father had recently experienced some heart trouble and had to take care. More than once he referred to himself as the 'senior citizen' in the company until, on one such occasion, Joe suddenly exclaimed loudly and dramatically, "Benjamin! you may be the senior citizen but *I* (Joseph) am your elder brother!". Martin Buber's I-Thou encounter had really come to pass. As Benjamin Bellet wrote to Irene afterwards: "It was a simple thought and yet psychologically profound because within minutes I became a member of your family. Joseph performed a miracle — within minutes I discovered what it takes many years or even a life-time of soul-searching to discover".

The wedding had been a time of exaltation of spirit and great family happiness. Less than a week later the morning post brought three letters of devastating rebuke and criticism, each related to a different issue which had arisen in the Diocese and on each of which Joe, after careful thought and prayer, had made his decision. This was a severe blow, felt the more deeply because of his weakened physical state. When the married couple returned to Salisbury from their brief honeymoon to spend a short period before flying out to America they found Joe in bed with excruciating pains in the chest.

The doctor thought it might be cramp but arranged for him

to go into hospital to be away from any diocesan calls. There, on July 2nd, he died, the post-mortem showing that there was an aneurysm of the aorta, a condition which, had it been known, would still have been inoperable. The treatment could only have been months in bed and slow decline. This was the cause of the physical symptoms which had dogged him since his first collapse: the official report of nervous exhaustion had been wide of the mark. The wonder was that for the last six months of his life he had carried on so bravely, often as though he had made a full recovery. Even more wonderful was his ability to preside over the wedding celebrations. The sadness in the days that followed can be forgotten. From the glory of the earthly celebration he went forward to the still greater glory of the heavenly reception.

13

The Agony and the Ecstasy

On the day after his death, Eric Heaton, now Dean of Christ Church, wrote this about him:

"Joe always struck me as a man who was only visiting this world — not in the sense that he didn't know to the full its agonies and its joys, but because his spirit was so clearly not bounded by them. It is this mysterious quality which made him for me, as for so many, a clue to what Christian faith is".

The agonies and the joys: not bounded. The agony was that of trying to break through every kind of bondage: the joy was that which comes from every sense of freedom.

He celebrated one of the critical moments of breakthrough by a lyric outburst: *Freedom and the Future.* Every new freedom brought new confidence for the future. And what was the essense of freedom? It was the ability to do one's own thing according to one's own vision of the best possible future — and that for Joe meant according to the will of God as he conceived it. He wanted always to move on. No achievement or position in his life could be regarded as absolute or final.

But this involved tension and, as has become clear from passages in his letters which I have quoted, one freedom which he struggled to achieve, but which by his own testimony he never finally attained, was psychological: he became increasingly aware that the abundance of loving concern which emanated from his early family circle was tending to suffocate him, was preventing him from establishing his own independence. He wanted to gain his own fulfilment through being related to a woman incarnating his own ideal and not necessarily conforming to that of his family's tradition.

But it was not only love-relationships which brought about a struggle for freedom. It was also the life of the intellect for, as Joe affirmed more than once, he had a *mind,* and that mind had to find a way forward which was free from self-deception and fear of others. From his early years he had been fascinated by the *history* of men and of nations: he knew that the true historian seeks to describe what really happened to the best of his ability. He had also been trained in the exact use of *language.* Further, when reading Greats at Oxford, he had been required to wrestle with Kant's *Fundamental Principles of the Metaphysic of Ethics.* "I strongly suspect after looking up my copy, that I never got beyond p 38. but I shall never forget the mental effort required even to get thus far". He had been made to *think.*

Thus far, the Bible had occupied a place apart in his intellectual exercises but when he began to read Theology, he was compelled to face historical, linguistic and, in a limited way, philosophical problems within what had hitherto been a sacred text. The views of his mother and of the Vicar of his home church and indeed of some of his closest friends in Oxford on these questions were well known to him. Could he break out into a new freedom of the intellect in which he could pursue these questions with integrity without throwing overboard the love for the Bible and the conviction that it bore witness to the revelation of God to mankind — a revelation which had become personal in his own experience through Jesus Christ? The crisis of freedom occurred when a Maltese boy confronted him with a simple question at the school in Cairo. But the breakthrough then was the culmination of a long process of inner questioning and the struggle had still to continue. He was free to examine afresh the Bible and the whole Christian tradition with his critical faculties. What parts had to be regarded as vitally relevant to life in the 20th. century? He could no longer feel bound by a stationary creed or by a religion which was "more of a camouflage or a crutch than the vital opening of the inner life".

There was one other major freedom to be achieved. This I can perhaps call the freedom of the life of worship. In the Evangelical tradition within which he had been nurtured there had often been a negative attitude to sacramental and liturgical forms of religion, a suspicion of symbols and symbolic acts as leading to idolatry. Joe never ceased to condemn idolatry though as he once declaimed: "The people at St. X Church think they have God taped on the altar while the people at St. Y Church think they have Him taped on the lectern". But neither sacramental nor liturgical forms need necessarily be idolatrous. The reading of Dom Gregory Dix's book *The Shape of the Liturgy* came to him as a revelation. "It transmitted the thrill of a eucharistically central church worship such as I had never experienced or read about before". Again this did not mean the end of the quest. Liturgical forms can become lifeless. Symbols can cease to quicken devotion. But once he had been released from the bondage of literalism, whether in relation to the Bible or to a particular form of worship, he went on to discover new treasures both in the Scriptures and in the manifold liturgical practices of Christendom.

Joe never attempted to become an expert on liturgical matters though he lectured on worship at the Ecumenical Institute in Bossey and tried there to redress the balance from what he regarded as an excessive emphasis on the Word. He welcomed the liturgical movement and approved of new experiments in worship being made in his own Church in the 60's. But there can be little doubt that his own major contribution to the Church of England, and indeed to the wider Church, was through his ministry of *the Word.* As prophet and evangelist, as expositor of the Old Testament and as witness to the good news in Christ Jesus he was supreme. Few men in our time have brought the Old Testament to life as he did: few have so persistently tried to bring everything, life and death, social issues and individual problems, ecclesiastical structures and secular affairs — to bring all into subjection to Christ.

The *secret* of his famous Bible-readings on the Old Testament, and particularly on Moses and the Exodus, is hard to define. He himself declared that George Adam Smith, through his books on Isaiah and the Twelve Prophets, first co-ordinated his heart and mind in Old Testament study. It is perhaps not without significance that Smith was able to write as vividly as he did because of his intimate knowledge of the Holy Land and its relation to other parts of the Middle East. Similarly Joe, through his five years spent in Egypt, his links with the Old Testament flavour of Ethiopic Christianity, and above all his two years of exploration of Jerusalem and its surroundings during the War, was able to bring familiar passages to new life and apply them to the cirumstances, political and individual, of our own time.

"I shall never forget" one of the chaplains wrote "standing at the gate of Samaria and hearing him read from Amos and describing some of the incidents from the Old Testament which happened there". He and his hearers were *there:* but not simply as re-enactors of the past but as applying that past to the world of the present. He could excite his audience because he had been excited himself when standing in the places where the prophets had been before.

Another key to his understanding of the Old Testament was undoubtedly his meeting with Martin Buber.

"I have been very greatly influenced by his books. In *Moses* he seems to me to write about the deepest reality of religion, as I know it, and to make coherent sense of it to me in a way no one else has done. If George Adam Smith showed me how Old Testament religion can be applied, Martin Buber opened my eyes to what it is''. Moses and the Burning Bush, Buber and his interpretation of 'I am that I am', the awe-struck cry 'He' — these became part and parcel of Joe's Bible expositions after 1944. His doctrine of God began not with logical arguments for God's existence but with a wondering and imaginative exclamation. Buber's interpretation so exactly met his own concern for freedom and and the future. God will be there in the future but not in the precise way in which I now see Him.

"Whether his (Buber's) exegesis of Exodus 3: 14 is sound or not, 'I shall be there as he who I there shall be' is superb in its demolition at one stroke of any mere subjective receptionism and of any mere objective ritualism''.

In such a theology Joe knew he could live.

I have suggested two influences which, by his own admission, helped him enormously in his exposition of the Old Testament. But there was still his own peculiar contribution which can only be described as the fruit of genius. It has been vividly portrayed in a letter written by Professor Owen Chadwick:

> I once heard him give lectures on the Book of Exodus. These lectures were the second best lectures I have ever heard on any Old Testament subject. But there was a peculiar feature of them. The Pentateuch is not generally regarded as an amusing subject of study. He had an audience of 100 almost hysterical with laughter for half-an-hour at a time. It was as entertaining as the performance of a top-class comedian. Yet there was not a moment of irreverence or inapropriateness. What was the gift that made this feat possible? *Gaiety* is a word not adequate to describe it. It was not *wit,* at least in the usual sense of that term. It was not superficial in any sense of mere playing to the gallery, and it left us all with the thought that we understood our Bibles better and valued the Old Testament more. I do not understand what the secret of this was. Anyone who tried to imitate it would certainly rush to a painful doom. I have no doubt that, whatever the secret was, it was something to do with the Christianity of his inmost soul.

With all his enthusiasm for the Old Testament and with all his veneration of Martin Buber, Joe never soft-pedalled his own conviction that in Christ God had revealed Himself in a way which altogether transcended even the greatest prophets' insights and expectations. It was not simply that a writer such as T. W. Manson had brought co-ordination to his heart and mind in the study of the New Testament. Rather it was that the figure of Jesus as portrayed in the Gospels had captivated him as the revelation of God so that no more challenging, no more exalted image could ever be imagined. He often quoted the Latin phrase which defines the cross as the touchstone of faith. It could be expanded to set forth Jesus in all his wods and deeds as the touchstone of all Joe's attempts to deal with the world of his own experience.

Yet the unanimous testimony of the New Testament writers was that the Cross did not mark the end. The willing acceptance of the Cross was the prelude to Pentecost, the most vivid illustration on the plane of history of what is a basic principle of the religious life. Only those who take up their cross willingly (which may be simply the very ordinary and humdrum circumstances of daily life) can expect to enjoy the blessing of the Spirit. "It was after Jesus had taken the decisive step of total identification to the uttermost with the traditional pattern of the lives of His sinful people and after he had gone down into the waters of John's baptism that He received the Holy Spirit on the other and yonder side of all human convention and custom and tradition".

The central aim of Joe's preaching was to bring his hearers face to face with *some* aspect of Jesus' career, expressed either through his words or through his actions. He returned again and again to one or other of his favourite passages: the birth at Bethlehem illustrating the divine strategy of starting precisely where people are: the boy Jesus amongst the doctors of the law illustrating the need 'to break the custom': the baptism in the Jordan illustrating Jesus' total identification with those he came to save: the eating with publicans and sinners illustrating Jesus' humanity and willingness to be misunderstood: the parable of the Good Samaritan illustrating Jesus' concern for the alien in race or class or religion: the parable of the Pharisee and the publican illustrating Jesus' condemnation of all hypocrisy and his approval of all honesty: and finally Gethsemane with the cry of agony and the Cross with the cry of dereliction. Joe rang the changes on these major incidents, calling upon his hearers to identify themselves with Jesus and thereby to receive the gift of the Holy Spirit.

This was the essence of his message but it gaind in power because of the *style* of its delivery. I do not think he had ever learned what were the most effective ways of holding attention and persuading to action. He constantly used the device of three sections and often made them memorable by alliterative headings. Magic, Mystery, Meaning; Credible, Creative, Crucified: Iconography, Iconolatry, Iconoclasm. Then his addresses abounded in contrasts: either/or: not this but that: they were full of concrete examples and references to the concerns of the day; they revealed his own involvement in whatever he was speaking about. There could suddenly be a thunder-clap or he would suddenly drop to a whisper. The discourse might be disordered, inconsequential, repetitive but it was alive, in deadly earnest and it often, by a clever juxtaposition of incongruous elements, produced an explosion of laughter. He never ceased to emphasize that self-effacement was the primary and authentic mark of the Spirit's activity: to point to Jesus was the hall-mark of a Spirit-possessed witness.

In February 1970 the Archbishop of Canterbury gave a course of four sermons on the Christian faith at Great St. Mary's Church in Cambridge. Joe was invited to preach on the following Sunday. His opening was entirely characteristic but strangly prophetic for it proved to be the last time that he stood in the pulpit associated with so many memories.

"Well, I thought of a text, 'There was a Pharaoh that arose that knew not Joseph', and I said to myself, 'Next time, (if I ever do have a next time here and I never probably shall) there will be a Vicar of Great St. Mary's who doesn't know me'. And I wondered, 'This is the end'. No, perhaps not. To-night, of course, it's a complete anti-climax; four University Sermons from the Archbishop and then *bathos*. Well 'Launch out into the *bathos* — the deep — that's the text''.

The picture of launching out into the deep was almost immediately complemented by a famous picture in one of John Oman's books: that of crossing a moor at night with some star perhaps to guide but with the need also for a lamp to direct the next step. Launching out into the deep, taking the next step — these were to be the basic themes of the sermon. They would be expressed, illustrated, given eternal significance by a vivid exposition of two incidents in Jesus' life, His baptism and His temptations.

Jesus going down to the Jordan, Jesus going out into the wilderness: Joe had often and often depicted the two scenes but this time there were all kinds of references to contemporary situations and experiences. In one sense he said nothing new and yet you never knew how he was going to treat his theme and what would come next. What he wanted above all for himself and for his hearers was that he and they should be identified with Jesus in taking the lowest place, whatever the act of self-humbling might involve and in joining with him in his temptations, again whatever that might imply for personal destiny. All this led him to the three alternative ways of living which were never far from his mind and imagination. No Cross — living for my own self-indulgence, My Cross — living for my own self-advertisement. God's Cross — living for God by self-sacrifice and a humble acceptance of His Will.

His final words were a moving conclusion of his preaching at Great St. Mary's, begun some 11 years previously. Through what the Archbishop had said there had come a vision of the distant outlines of the hills on the horizon.

"But you must take the next step on the path across the moor. And you walk by faith and not by sight. It seems to me that the step may be *down* into the river to accept the ministrations of John the Baptist — whatever that means for me to-day; or it may be *out* into the wilderness to test the principles to which baptism committed me . . . The next step can be either along that marked No Cross or along that marked My Cross or along that marked God's Cross. If it is the last we have a companion with us and we may hear him say as he said to his friends long ago 'Ye are they which have continued with me in my temptations'. 'I am with you always even unto the end of the world'''.

III

I suppose the most searching questions that have been asked about Joe's career are: Was it right for those in authority to offer him the appointment as bishop of a large rural diocese? Was it right for him to accept? The doubts found vivid expression in a metaphor which appeared in *The Times* obituary:

"When his appointment to the see of Salisbury was announced many of his friends thought that a racehorse was being harnessed to the shafts of a farm wagon".

A friend over many years was Max Warren who, in 1972, was soon to retire from his canonry at Westminster. Max corresponded regularly with his daughter and son-in-law who were in India and on the day after reading of Joe's death he wrote:

"Perhaps the most truly prophetic person I have ever had the privilege to know, a man of most radiant if explosive personality, he was warmhearted and an uncompromising optimist based on his deep assurance of his Gospel. A wiser leadership in the Church and more perceptiveness on his part, would have held him to being a teacher of theology in a theological college. There his magnificent grasp of the Bible and his integrity and his ability to relate the Bible to the contemporary world would have fired generations of young men and the Church to-day would have a large number of clergy who would be relevant and prophetic without jumping on to the bandwagon of the latest fad. Alas! he was allowed to go to Great St. Mary's, Cambridge to succeed Mervyn Stockwood. This was not his fault. Then for some astonishing reason he was made Bishop of Salisbury, a diocese of hundreds of tiny villages, Hardy country for most part, in which his genius for the unexpected remark was right above the heads of clergy and people. I think the strain of this unnatural occupation killed him.

"Years ago in a News-Letter I pleaded that if a man was a good teacher of theology there was no higher vocation than being on the staff of a theological college. I was utterly dismayed by the way in which good Africans from theological colleges assumed that becoming a bishop represented promotion. What nonsense. Being a bishop is a vocation of a totally different kind, a form of crucifixion, to be endured only by rare characters who can adorn this ministry, or such as have the humbler gifts, none the less holy, of pastoral concern and some capacity for devolution. Only very rarely is a modern bishop competent as a theologian or capable of prophesying without talking nonsense.

"Well dear Joe has gone to receive a 'Well done, good and faithful servant'. He was certainly good and enormously faithful. But he was in a category by himself. To-day there is no 'open vision' and the voice of prophecy is silent".

And later Max wrote in his diary: "Joe was too sensitive and self-questioning to fit in at Salisbury".

Max Warren was one of the shrewdest commentators within the Church of England but he was not infallible and he had his own particular views about the episcopate! It is highly doubtful whether Joe could ever have remained within an English theological college as it is structured to-day: he would have been like an eagle in a cage. And he was not only a prophet. It was a most notable feature of his two-sided personality that he was also a most sensitive and compassionate pastor. Could he have had more extensive opportunities for pastoral concern than he had in the city and diocese of Salisbury?

Another friend and wise observer was Professor C. F. D. Moule. In a sermon preached at Great St. Mary's in 1978 he reflected on Joe's gifts. He first compared him to Jeremiah, a man "with a passionate sense of his irresistible mission; his message was like a fire blazing in his heart: he could not hold it in". He might, Professor Moule suggested, have made a success of a good many different things: he could have been an actor or a 'cogent theological specialist'. But he heard God's call to be a Pastor, "with a tender concern to bring individuals to wholeness and to their full stature as children of God in the Gospel of Christ" and a Prophet, "vivacious, electrifying, bold, rash, even tactless — he must speak out with courage what he knew to be God's message".

Then, however came this passage in the sermon. "The Church (I think many of us feel) ought to have a niche for Prophets. It was a tragedy that a person with the gifts and calling of Joe Fison should be harassed and worn down with administrative business and shackled by convention — not that the strongest convention could wholly subdue one so unconventional! But he ought to have been free to be God's actor in the finest sense — God's fool (how often Joe delighted to quote St. Paul: 'I speak as a fool'), God's jester, if you like — bringing the drama and the pathos and the joy of the Gospel home in his inimitable way to hosts of listeners.

"Yet, as it was, nobody can say that he failed: nobody can call him, like Jeremiah, tragic. Even those who were sad that he was shackled by tasks that he ought to have been spared, agreed that, through them, he brought them near to God. His passionate love for his Lord and for all his fellow-beings shone through the weariness and the toil. And above all, it was his Lord's humility that infused even his most devastating words and deeds".

Such were the observations of two long-term friends who could view his appointment to the episcopate with a certain detachment. But were they right in their judgments and their reservations? What *could* be powerfully argued is that the diocese of Salisbury, with its traditional structure, was not one in which Joe's particular gifts could be most fruitfully exercised. His challenging voice might have sounded out to greater effect in a diocese containing centres of learning or of the arts or of industry though that is not certain. What is more to the point is that a diocese covering the county of Dorset and most of Wiltshire was too large to enable him to exercise his pastoral gift in the way he wanted to do. It is significant that as part of his Visitation Charge in 1970 he frankly admitted that the Bishop must be responsible for fewer clergy "if he is to have any really personal and intimate knowledge of them". Further, even with fewer clergy, the personal ministry could only be effective if some of the administrative responsibilities could be shed. Yet he could not see himself as called to preside over the dissolution of the Diocese. Here was the dilemma. The impossibility of fulfilling what he most wanted to do within the structure now existing: the impossibility of changing the structure without spending years in organising a constitutional reform. This was part of the agony involved in being Bishop of Salisbury. Yet who can deny that he also found the job exciting, fascinating and in countless ways fulfilling?

I suspect that in the depths of his own heart he regarded this final phase of his career as God's Cross. He did not seek it: it came to him as a surprise: he might have wished for something else, though, apart from the possibility of some other diocese, it is not easy to see what that something else could have been. He was convinced that if it was God's Cross for him then he must take it up with joy for only by way of Calvary could the blessing of the Holy Spirit be experienced within any social context.

Perhaps the area in which he felt the greatest frustration, in which he sensed something of 'the sufferings of Christ', was in the resistance to change which he so often encountered. When he was appointed, a letter from a friend expressed the hope that he, whose vocation it had hitherto been 'to set theological cats among ecclesiastical pigeons', would now "shun the cope of episcopal caution and continue as a prophet of the highest". Another hoped that he would give the diocese "a shot in the arm". And in a report to the Diocese he claimed that the most significant thing to have been said at the Lambeth Conference in 1968 were the words of the Bishop of Iran when he spoke about the perils of disunity:

"Over and above the historic divisions and differences in the Church, a new, subtle and dangerous cleavage is appearing, cutting across the ancient denominations. This is the difference between those who are struggling to find new ways to interpret the Gospel for modern man and those who sit tightly in their familiar corners and oppose any kind of change".

Joe tried always to understand, to sympathize, to make allowances for special circumstances. But wherever there was a dour determination to dig the heels in and refuse to consider any kind of change or advance he was torn between agony and indignation. How could such an attitude be reconciled with the ringing words of the last book of the Bible: 'Behold I make all things new'?.

As a final judgment on his episcopate I quote some words written by John Baker, who was consecrated Bishop of Salisbury in 1982, nearly ten years after Joe's death:

"Bishop George Reindorp said to me when talking about the diocese before I came here: 'I followed a saint but a saint who kept no files'. Files or no files it was Joe's burning, loving holiness that mattered, his living within the vision of God and in obedience to Christ I can tesify that of all the twentieth century Bishops of Salisbury he is the one that is most remembered, his name is the one that is most often mentioned with love, laughter and admiration from Lyme Regis to Wootton Bassett. Those who say it was wrong to send him should ponder these things.''

IV

Let me conclude these reflections on Joe's particular qualities by quoting tributes by his own children to what their father meant to them:

The first is by Flint, his elder son:

''My father may have been upset at some of his family's failures to conform to traditional Christian morals and vitues — for instance my general laziness and in particular as to churchgoing and my carelessness about tidiness. He may have suffered from what church people would think but he was never angry about this or told us we had to keep up appearances.

''As against these difficulties, the freedom he and my mother gave us meant we could try to work out our interpretation to life which was true for ourselves and not just a framework suggested from outside. And I (and maybe my brothers and sisters) could, unlike many of my contemporaries, retain my childhood impressions of a loving God and develop my own experience of Him in my life without being put off religion by seeing it as a requirement of conformity''.

The second is by Marianne, his younger daughter:

''He made a great impression on friends I brought home — especially the non-Christians. I personally, when I was having periods of agnosticism, came to use him as an example. My reasoning was like this. If Daddy is so fired by his belief in God and Christ and so excited by it, surely there must be something in it. He can't just be believing in a figure of the imagination.

''Towards the last months of his life he definitely seemed to me to be drifting away. He didn't seem to be interested in things. At the time of his death I just happened to be at Evensong in Exeter Cathedral and I had the most extraordinary feeling of well-being. The choir sang an anthem 'Be strong'. After that I had to go into the hospital as I was on call that weekend and I was in a sort of happy dream. It wasn't until I got back to my flat later that I learnt that Daddy had died at the same time as the service was on. I couldn't be sad — just very relieved for Daddy. I think we all felt that. Certainly those feelings in the Cathedral were of a *very* special sort. They were incredibly melancholically happy is how I'd describe them and

141

they were not feelings I imagined I had had once I learnt that Daddy had died''.

14

A burning and a shining light

On the day after Joe died an ex-headmaster wrote to Irene:

"Every memory of Joe is vital and vivid. He is one of those men whom no one who met him, however briefly, will ever forget. I can see you both as clearly as I can see the room about me now when we met first. You were at Truro then and came to ask some questions about Flint's entry. I seem to think there was a brilliant sunshine coming through the window of my little office but it may have been just the sunshine of Joe's presence there.

"We were on the same wave-length in half a minute and a friendship began which will fortify me all my days. Here was a man who was wholly *good:* his heart and mind were filled with Christ's love and from him came an infection of goodness which gave warmth and light to us ordinary chaps: this didn't just die: it goes on living to enlighten all our lives.

"And what *fun* he was. Every meeting with him was a joy. The Close will never be quite the same for me. But I shall see him and hear him in countless places. Nor will his friends ever forget his courage and cheerfulness in the last year or two when so many physical ills were coming upon him.

"We all loved him".

This spontaneous tribute is typical of hundreds of letters which came to Irene and to Joe's sister Kathleen after his death. *Warmth* and *Light: the Fire* and *the Lamp* and Fire in the first place. He was a man of Fire. He was fascinated by the bush that burned with fire and was not consumed. He felt a particular empathy with Jeremiah, for whom God's Word, imprisoned in his body was "like a Fire blazing in my heart". Above all his inner being was grasped by and responded to the cry of Jesus:

I came to cast fire upon the earth;

And how I wish it was now kindled.

He chose *Fire upon the earth* as the title of what could be regarded as his most moving and most characteristic book.

Fire is an ambivalent symbol. It can warm but it can also scorch. It can purify but it can also destroy. And those who are near it may enjoy its blessings or they may seek to quench it or flee from it. In trying to give a record of Joe's life I have said little about the latter aspect for there can be little doubt that in his ministry it was the former of which men and women were most aware and which they most eagerly welcomed.

For example, a minister of the Church of Scotland, who had

known Joe as a Chaplain in Jerusalem, wrote to him some years after he had lectured at the Aberdeen Kirk Week:

"I heard great accounts of your work at the Aberdeen Kirk Week a few years ago. In fact I owe you a debt of gratitude, for two of my most 'difficult' elders came back from that and set fire to the rest of my Kirk Session. It was a goodly blaze! The results, I believe, are still to be seen on Clydeside".

But there were also those who disagreed with Joe, criticized him and in a few cases tried to quench his flaming spirit. *The Times* obituary did not disguise the fact that he had his 'detractors', that he made many 'gaffes' and that he could arouse indignation amongst those who only knew him slightly and expected different behaviour from a bishop.

He may have been over-enthusiastic, he may have tried to ride rough shod over traditional proprieties, he may have been too eager to summon the winds of change to come from the four corners of the earth and blow upon the Salisbury diocese, he may have tended to underestimate the width of the generation gap, he may have been too quick to jump to conclusions. Yet when all this is said the fact remains that he was always ready to criticize himself and never allowed criticism from others, however much he might feel it, to extinguish the fire of his own love for 'the brother for whom Christ died'. I can only give my personal testimony to the effect that I have never read more obviously heartfelt and deeply sincere appreciations of any man than those which poured in after his death.

From that of Archbishop Michael Ramsey who described him as 'God's lovely gift' to that of the little girl who said when she heard the news, "Oh dear, he was so kind to me": from the Sister in the Convent of the Epiphany in Truro who remembered visiting with Joe one of the poorest homes in the town and seeing him immediately winnng the confidence of a distraught mother, to a Congregationalist minister who remembered how Joe used to go to endless trouble in ecumenical gatherings to 'include in' all who were not of his own communion and how in particular he upheld this man by his prayers after he had undergone an operation: from the Headmaster who affirmed that "just through the medium of perhaps four or five hand-written letters I had the most wonderful sense not merely of human understanding and sympathy but of spiritual support", to the man who, as a sixth-former, had wondered whether a "vital Christianity and a mature intellect were really compatible" and who, at that time, had first been convinced by what he saw in Joe that this was indeed the case: from the Vicar who "disagreed with him deeply on a number of things. But the wonderful thing was that you could disagree with him in the most uncompromising terms and yet be very conscious at the same time that you still had the deepest things of all in common and so be unaffectedly united in prayers together after your discussion", to another who described him as "a Bishop born for an age when every aspect of tradition is under fire. Far from deploring such a situation he advanced to meet it, flags flying and bugles blowing, confident in the ultimate victory of the Gospel": from Sir Owen Morshead, Chairman of the Dorset Historic Churches Trust who described him as "the most outgiving man I ever met", to the widow of Joe's one-time chauffeur who wrote to Kathleen: "There was a wonderful affinity of mind and spirit between the Bishop and my husband. Your Brother was the most wonderful person I have ever met and must have shouldered the burdens of hundreds of people (including me) throughout his life-time": from all ranks and from all kinds of affiliations came expressions of esteem, gratitude and affection.

Nothing could have been more fitting as a public tribute than the great Service of Thanksgiving in Salisbury Cathedral twelve days after his death. It was estimated that a crowd of 2,500 was present in the building which he had come to love: on opening the service sheet they found a single quotation on two otherwise blank pages. It had so often been on Joe's lips expressing the dual, the dialectical character of his own understanding of God and of His relation to the world.

> The bird on the branch, the lily in the meadow, the stag in the forest, the fish in the sea, the countless joyful creatures sing, God is love. But beneath all these sopranos, as it were a sustained bass part, sounds the *De profundis* of the Sacrificed, God is love.

The opening hymn, sung to Handel's stirring tune, was a shout of joy. "Thine is the glory, risen conquering Son". The moment was one of the most dramatic I have ever experienced. The final line of the chorus

> 'Endless is the vict'ry thou o'er death has won'

set the tone for the whole service. Jeremy Walsh, one of Joe's assistants at Great St. Mary's, who had become Rector of Marlborough, preached the sermon. He gave thanks for Joe's warm *humanity,* for all that he taught us about *humility,* and for the *hope* that was at the heart of his proclamation of the Christian Gospel.

He concluded with this tribute;

> Immense affection, born of the love of God within him;

sincere humility, learned through his deep understanding of the humility of Christ and a firm hope, born of trust in the active and unconquerable power of the living God. These things mark no easy, carefree way of life. You cannot care without suffering agonies, you cannot be humble without being aware of your failures; you cannot hope for resurrection without first accepting the Cross, and finding resurrection only on the *yonder* side".

The great thanksgiving ended with the Blessing given in words used by Joe at his enthronement and then, Irene and her family, the intimate circle within which Joe had found constant support, refreshment and love, entertained relations, and friends from a distance, in the spirit of confidence and hope which Joe himself would have inspired on such an occasion.

II

I have spoken of Joe's *penchant* for alliteration. Amongst the tributes and memories in letters, sermons, parish magazines and newspapers the words *humanity* and *humility* appear again and again. "His humanity" Mr. Michael Hamilton wrote in The Times "was never disciplined. The illness of a friend, the problem of Rhodesia, the day-to-day crises of a troubled world — he could never stand aside from these things. With each and every issue he deliberately chose to become deeply and personally committed". And humanity for him meant the recognition that all mankind were included within the outreach of God's love. 'The middle wall of partition' was to him a symbol of anti-Christ: in and through His Cross, Christ had created a new humanity, and it was a humanity without barriers that Joe himself sought constantly to bring into being.

There were even more testimonies to his *humility* than to his humanity. So rare a virtue, it was said, yet one which radiated from him in an utterly natural way. The secret of it, I suggest, may be found in two other qualities, each beginning with the letter 'h'. The first was his complete *honesty*. How he fulminated againt hypocrisy, pretense, humbug, escapism, subterfuges, masks, dodges, camouflage. How frequently he quoted Robert Burns:

O wad some Pow'r the giftie gie us
To see oursels as other see us!

He simply could not hide his opinions or his feelings. He once exclaimed: "A Religion that is not honest is no real religion at all". He was willing to be vulnerable because he was willing to be fully known.

The lawyer Alfieri's moving words at the end of Arthur

Miller's play, *A View from the Bridge*, have often come to my mind when thinking of Joe. Alfieri is speaking of Eddie who has just met a violent death. In many ways Eddie was a very different character from Joe but he *"allowed himself to be wholly known"*.

"Most of the time now we settle for half . . . But the truth is holy and even as I know how wrong he was . . . I tremble, for I confess that something perversely pure calls to me from his memory — not purely good, but himself purely, for he allowed himself to be wholly known and for that I think I will love him more than all my sensible clients".

Besides his honesty there was his *humour*. Never ostentatious, never cruel, never trivial — it was just irrepressible. Yet it was not a thing apart from the rest of his character for he was never at home with straightforward logic, with the single vision, with the tame over-simplification. Instead he lived in tension between two poles, in dialectical interchange, in the juxtaposition of opposites, and again and again it was the very bringing together of apparent incompatibilities which sparked off the laughter. The brilliant word of reconciliation was used not only in preaching the gospel but also in joining together the oddest factors in human experience. He could have been a comic actor. Instead he united matters of deadly seriousness with bursts of tremendous fun. Who except Joe would ever have dared to say:

"What the Almighty must think about this is quite unprintable!".

His honesty and his humour made him both human and humble. I want to add one more 'h'. It is a word that one does not use lightly though it frequently appeared in Joe's own vocabulary. He wrote about holy places, holy people, holy writings, the holy city. But the word also appeared in the testimonies to what people felt in Joe's presence: he was a *holy* man.

He grew up in home surroundings where holiness was regarded as the supreme blessing within the life of religion. It might be striven for, it might be freely bestowed. It was held up as the pearl of great price. Joe learned later to appreciate the works of Catholic writers on the nature of spirituality and recognized the value of disciplined prayer and acts of devotion. He also came to realise that certain aspects of evangelical piety could degenerate into sentimentalism and self-deception.

Yet in 1958, both in an article for *The Expository Times* describing his intellectual and spiritual pilgrimage, and as introduction to his book *Fire upon the Earth,* he fastened upon a poem by Amy Carmichael, missionary and founder of a Children's Home in South India, as expressing a piety "as nearly Christlike as anything I have ever known". The poem seems to embody Joe's highest aspirations and many came to see in him the actual manifestation of that holiness which was the object of his prayer.

From prayer that asks that I may be
Sheltered from winds that beat on Thee,
From fearing when I should aspire,
From faltering when I should climb higher,
From silken self, O Captain, free
Thy soldier who would follow Thee.

From subtle love of softening things,
From easy choices, weakenings,
(Not thus are spirits fortified,
Not this way went the Crucified)
From all that dims Thy Calvary,
O Lamb of God, deliver me.

Give me the love that leads the way,
The faith that nothing can dismay,
The hope no disappointments tire,
The passion that will burn like fire,
Let me not sink to be a clod:
Make me Thy fuel, Flame of God.

"The scholar-saint of our generation" one called him. Let the final word be that of Father Harry Williams, who, writing to Joe from Trinity College when he learned of his appointment to Salisbury said:

"For the Church of England I am absolutely delighted. It couldn't be better news. But we shall miss you here more than I can say.

"Of your many gifts it is not necessary to write. But I would like to tell you how, when in your presence, I have always felt strongly the presence of our Lord".

Joe's own last word might have been the phrase which he taught others to add to the traditional prayer:

"May the souls of the departed rest in peace:"
And rise in Glory.